NEW
PERSPECTIVES
S E R I E S

Microsoft®
Windows® 95

INTRODUCTORY

The New Perspectives Series

The New Perspectives Series consists of texts and technology that teach computer concepts and the programs listed below. Both Windows 3.1 and Windows 95 versions of these programs are available. You can order these New Perspectives texts in many different lengths, software releases, bound combinations, CourseKits™ and Custom Editions. Contact your CTI sales representative or customer service representative for the most up-to-date details.

The New Perspectives Series

Computer Concepts®

dBASE®

Internet/World Wide Web/Netscape Navigator®

Lotus 1-2-3®

Microsoft Access®

Microsoft Excel®

Microsoft Office Professional®

Microsoft PowerPoint®

Microsoft Windows 3.1®

Microsoft Windows 95®

Microsoft Word®

Microsoft Works®

Novell Perfect Office®

Paradox®

Presentations®

Quattro Pro®

WordPerfect®

Microsoft® Windows® 95

INTRODUCTORY

June Jamrich Parsons
University of the Virgin Islands

Dan Oja
GuildWare, Inc.

A Susan Solomon Book

CTI

A DIVISION OF COURSE TECHNOLOGY
ONE MAIN STREET, CAMBRIDGE, MA 02142

an International Thomson Publishing company I(T)P

Albany • Bonn • Boston • Cambridge • Cincinnati • London • Madrid • Melbourne
Mexico City • New York • Paris • San Francisco • Singapore • Tokyo • Toronto • Washington

New Perspectives on Microsoft Windows 95—Introductory is published by CTI.

Managing Editor	Mac Mendelsohn
Series Consulting Editor	Susan Solomon
Product Manager	Susan Solomon
Production Editor	Debbie Masi
Text and Cover Designer	Ella Hanna
Cover Illustrator	Nancy Nash

© 1996 by CTI.
A Division of Course Technology—I(T)P

For more information contact:

Course Technology
One Main Street
Cambridge, MA 02142

International Thomson Publishing Europe
Berkshire House 168-173
High Holborn
London WCIV 7AA
England

Thomas Nelson Australia
102 Dodds Street
South Melbourne, 3205
Victoria, Australia

Nelson Canada
1120 Birchmount Road
Scarborough, Ontario
Canada M1K 5G4

International Thomson Editores
Campos Eliseos 385, Piso 7
Col. Polanco
11560 Mexico D.F. Mexico

International Thomson Publishing GmbH
Kônigswinterer Strasse 418
53227 Bonn
Germany

International Thomson Publishing Asia
211 Henderson Road
#05-10 Henderson Building
Singapore 0315

International Thomson Publishing Japan
Hirakawacho Kyowa Building, 3F
2-2-1 Hirakawacho
Chiyoda-ku, Tokyo 102
Japan

Trademarks
Course Technology and the open book logo are registered trademarks of Course Technology.
I(T)P The ITP logo is a trademark under license.
Microsoft and Windows 95 are registered trademarks of Microsoft Corporation.

Some of the product names and company names used in this book have been used for identification purposes only and may be trademarks or registered trademarks of their respective manufacturers and sellers.

Disclaimer
CTI reserves the right to revise this publication and make changes from time to time in its content without notice.

ISBN 0-7600-3489-3

Printed in the United States of America

10 9 8 7

At CTI, we have one foot in education and the other in technology. We believe that technology is transforming the way people teach and learn, and we are excited about providing instructors and students with materials that use technology to teach about technology.

Our development process is unparalleled in the higher education publishing industry. Every product we create goes through an exacting process of design, development, review, and testing.

Reviewers give us direction and insight that shape our manuscripts and bring them up to the latest standards. Every manuscript is quality tested. Students whose backgrounds match the intended audience work through every keystroke, carefully checking for clarity and pointing out errors in logic and sequence. Together with our own technical reviewers, these testers help us ensure that everything that carries our name is error-free and easy to use.

We show both *how* and *why* technology is critical to solving problems in college and in whatever field you choose to teach or pursue. Our time-tested, step-by-step instructions provide unparalleled clarity. Examples and applications are chosen and crafted to motivate students.

As the New Perspectives Series team at CTI, our goal is to produce the most timely, accurate, creative, and technologically sound product in the entire college publishing industry. We strive for consistent high quality. This takes a lot of communication, coordination, and hard work. But we love what we do. We are determined to be the best. Write us and let us know what you think. You can also e-mail us at info@course.com.

The New Perspectives Series Team

Joseph Adamski	Jessica Evans	Dan Oja
Judy Adamski	Kathy Finnegan	June Parsons
Roy Ageloff	Robin Geller	Sandra Poindexter
David Auer	Roger Hayen	Ann Shaffer
Rachel Bunin	Charles Hommel	Susan Solomon
Joan Carey	Chris Kelly	Christine Spillett
Patrick Carey	Terry Ann Kremer	Susanne Walker
Barbara Clemens	Melissa Lima	John Zeanchock
Kim Crowley	Nancy Ludlow	Beverly Zimmerman
Kristen Duerr	Mac Mendelsohn	Scott Zimmerman

Preface The New Perspectives Series

What is the New Perspectives Series?

CTI's **New Perspectives Series** is an integrated system of instruction that combines text and technology products to teach computer concepts and microcomputer applications. Users consistently praise this series for innovative pedagogy, creativity, supportive and engaging style, accuracy, and use of interactive technology. The first New Perspectives text was published in January of 1993. Since then, the series has grown to more than 40 titles and has become the best-selling series on computer concepts and microcomputer applications. Others have imitated the New Perspectives features, design, and technologies, but none have replicated its quality and its ability to consistently anticipate and meet the needs of instructors and students.

What is the Integrated System of Instruction?

You hold in your hands a textbook that is one component of an integrated system of instruction—text, graphics, video, sound animation, and simulations that are linked and that provide a flexible, unified, and interactive system to help you teach and help your students learn. Specifically, the *New Perspectives Integrated System of Instruction* consists of five components: a Course Technology textbook, Course Labs, Course Online, Course Presenter, and Course Test Manager. These components—shown in the graphic on the back cover of this book—have been developed to work together to provide a complete, integrative teaching and learning experience.

How is the New Perspectives Series different from other microcomputer applications series?

The **New Perspectives Series** distinguishes itself from other series in at least four substantial ways: sound instructional design, consistent quality, innovative technology, and proven pedagogy. The texts in this series consist of two or more tutorials, which are based on sound instructional design. Each tutorial is motivated by a realistic case that is meaningful to students. Rather than learn a laundry list of features, students learn the features in the context of solving a problem. This process motivates all concepts and skills by demonstrating to students why they would want to know them.

Instructors and students have come to rely on the high quality of the **New Perspectives Series** and to consistently praise its accuracy. This accuracy is a result of CTI's unique multi-step quality assurance process that incorporates student testing at three stages of development, using hardware and software configurations appropriate to the product. All solutions, test questions, and other Course Tools (see below) are tested using similar procedures. Instructors who adopt this series report that students can work through the tutorials independently, with a minimum of intervention or "damage control" by instructors or staff. This consistent quality has meant that if instructors are pleased with one product from the series, they can rely on the same quality with any other New Perspectives product.

The **New Perspectives Series** also distinguishes itself by its innovative technology. This series innovated Course Labs, truly *interactive* learning applications. These have set the standard for interactive learning.

How do I know that the New Perspectives Series will work?

Some instructors who use this series report a significant difference between how much their students learn and retain with this series as compared to other series. With other series, instructors often find that students can work through the book and do well on homework and tests, but still not demonstrate competency when asked to perform particular tasks outside the context of the text's sample case or project. With the **New Perspectives Series**, however, instructors report that students have a complete, integrative learning experience that stays with them. They credit this high retention and competency to the fact that this series incorporates critical thinking and problem solving with computer skills mastery.

How does this book I'm holding fit into the New Perspectives Series?

New Perspectives microcomputer applications books are available in the following categories:

Brief books are about 100 pages long and are intended to teach only the essentials of the particular microcomputer application.

Introductory books are about 300 pages long and consist of 6 or 7 tutorials. An Introductory book is designed for a short course on a particular application or for a one-term course to be used in combination with other introductory books. The book you are holding is an Introductory book.

Comprehensive books consist of all of the tutorials in the Introductory book, plus 3 or 4 more tutorials on more advanced topics. They also include Brief Windows tutorials, 3 or 4 Additional Cases, and a Reference Section.

Advanced books begin by covering topics similar to those in the Comprehensive books, but cover them in more depth. Advanced books then go on to present the most high-level coverage in the series.

Concepts *New Perspectives on Computer Concepts* is available in Brief, Introductory, Comprehensive, and chapter-by-chapter versions.

Custom Books offer you two ways to customize the New Perspectives Series to fit your course exactly: *CourseKits*, 2 or more texts packaged together in a box, and *Custom Editions*, your choice of books bound together. Both options offer significant price discounts.

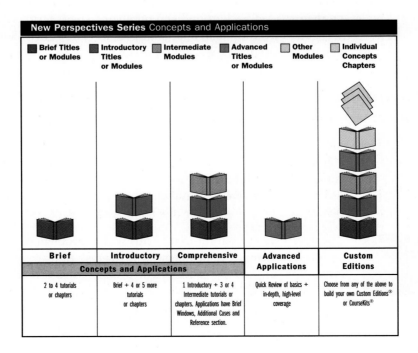

	New Perspectives Series Concepts and Applications				
■ Brief Titles or Modules	■ Introductory Titles or Modules	■ Intermediate Modules	■ Advanced Titles or Modules	□ Other Modules	□ Individual Concepts Chapters
Brief	**Introductory**	**Comprehensive**	**Advanced Applications**	**Custom Editions**
Concepts and Applications				
2 to 4 tutorials or chapters	Brief + 4 or 5 more tutorials or chapters	1 Introductory + 3 or 4 Intermediate tutorials or chapters. Applications have Brief Windows, Additional Cases and Reference section.	Quick Review of basics + in-depth, high-level coverage	Choose from any of the above to build your own Custom Editions® or CourseKits®

In what kind of course could I use this book?

You can use this book in any course in which you want students to learn the most important Microsoft Windows 95 topics, including basic navigation and file management skills. It is particularly recommended for a short course on Windows 95. This book assumes students have no previous experience with Windows 95.

How do the Windows 95 editions differ from the Windows 3.1 editions?

Larger Page Size If you've used a New Perspectives text before, you'll immediately notice that the book you're holding is larger than the Windows 3.1 series books. We've responded to user requests for a larger page, which allows for larger screen shots and associated callouts. Look on page WIN95 24 for an example of how we've made the screen shots easier to read.

Sessions We've divided the tutorials into sessions. Each session is designed to be completed in about 45 minutes to an hour (depending, of course, upon student needs and the speed of your lab equipment). With sessions, learning is broken up into more easily-assimilated chunks. You can more accurately allocate time in your syllabus. Students can better manage the available lab time. Each session begins with a "session box," which quickly describes the skills students will learn in the session. Furthermore, each session is numbered, which makes it easier for you and your students to navigate and communicate about the tutorial. Look on page WIN95 30 for the session box that opens Session 21.

Quick Checks Each session concludes with meaningful, conceptual questions—called Quick Checks—that test students' understanding of what they learned in the session. Answers to all of the Quick Checks are at the back of the book preceding the Index. You can find examples of Quick Checks on pages WIN95 13 and 25.

New Design We have retained the best of the old design to help students differentiate between what they are to *do* and what they are to *read*. The steps are clearly identified by their shaded background and numbered steps. Furthermore, this new design presents steps and screen shots in a larger, easier to read format. Some good examples of our new design are pages WIN95 64 and 65.

What features are retained in the Windows 95 editions of the New Perspectives Series?

"Read This Before You Begin" Page This page is consistent with CTI's unequaled commitment to helping instructors introduce technology into the classroom. Technical considerations and assumptions about hardware and software are listed in one place to help instructors save time and eliminate unnecessary aggravation. The "Read This Before You Begin" page for this book is on page WIN95 2.

Tutorial Case Each tutorial begins with a problem presented in a case that is meaningful to students. The problem turns the task of learning how to use an application into a problem-solving process. The problems increase in complexity with each tutorial. These cases touch on multicultural, international, and ethical issues—so important to today's business curriculum. See page WIN95 57 for the case that begins Tutorial 3.

1.
2.
3.

Step-by-Step Methodology This unique CTI methodology keeps students on track. They enter data, click buttons, or press keys always within the context of solving the problem posed in the tutorial case. The text constantly guides students, letting them know where they are in the course of solving the problem. In addition, the numerous screen shots include callouts that direct students' attention to what they should look at on the screen. On almost every page in this book, you can find an example of how steps, screen shots, and callouts work together.

TROUBLE?

TROUBLE? Paragraphs These paragraphs anticipate the mistakes or problems that students are likely to have and help them recover and continue with the tutorial. By putting these paragraphs in the book, rather than in the Instructor's Manual, we facilitate independent learning and free the instructor to focus on substantive conceptual issues rather than on common procedural errors. Two representative examples of Trouble?s are on pages WIN95 32 and 33.

Reference Windows Reference Windows appear throughout the text. They are succinct summaries of the most important tasks covered in the tutorials. Reference Windows are specially designed and written so students can use them for their reference value when doing the Tutorial Assignments and Case Problems, and after completing the course. Page WIN95 67 contains the Reference Window for Renaming a Folder.

Task Reference The Task Reference is a summary of how to perform common tasks using the most efficient method, as well as helpful shortcuts. It appears as a table at the end of the book. In this book the Task Reference is on pages WIN95 157 to 160.

Tutorial Assignments, Case Problems, and Lab Assignments Each tutorial concludes with a Tutorial Assignment, which provides students additional hands-on practice of the skills they learned in the tutorial. The Tutorial Assignment is followed by four Case Problems that have approximately the same scope as the tutorial case. In the Windows 95 applications texts, there is always one Case Problem in the book and one in the Instructor's Manual that require students to solve the problem independently, with minimum guidance. Finally, if a Lab (see below) accompanies the tutorial, a Lab Assignment is included. Look on pages WIN95 141 through 144 for the Tutorial Assignments for Tutorial 4. The Lab Assignments for Tutorial 3 are on page WIN95 93.

Exploration Exercises The Windows environment allows students to learn by exploring and discovering what they can do. Exploration Exercises can be Tutorial Assignments or Case Problems that might challenge students, encourage them to explore the capabilities of the program they are using, and extend their knowledge using the Windows Help facility and other reference materials. Page WIN95 92 contains Exploration Exercises for Tutorial 3.

The New Perspectives Series is known for using technology to help instructors teach and administer, and to help students learn. What CourseTools are available with this textbook?

All of the teaching and learning materials available with the **New Perspectives Series** are known as CourseTools. Most of them are available in the Instructor's Resource Kit.

Course Labs: Now, Concepts Come to Life   Computer skills and concepts come to life with the New Perspectives Course Labs—highly interactive tutorials that combine illustrations, animations, digital images, and simulations. The Labs guide students step-by-step, present them Quick Checks, allow them to explore on their own, test their comprehension, and provide printed feedback. Lab Assignments are included at the end of each relevant tutorial. The Labs available with this book and the tutorials in which they appear are:

Using a Keyboard	Tutorial 1
Using a Mouse	Tutorial 1
Using Files	Tutorial 2
Windows Directories, Folders, and Files	Tutorial 3

Course Online: A site Dedicated to Keeping You and Your Students Up-To-Date   When you use a New Perspectives product, you can access CTI's faculty and student sites on the World Wide Web. You may browse the password-protected Faculty Online Companion to obtain all the materials you need to prepare for class. Please see your Instructor's Manual or call your Course Technology customer service representative for more information. Students may access their Online Companion in the Student Center using the URL http://www.vmedia.com/cti/.

Course Presenter: Ready-Made or Customized Dynamic Presentations
Course Presenter is a CD-ROM-based presentation tool that provides instructors with a wealth of resources for use in the classroom, replacing traditional overhead transparencies with computer-generated screenshows. Course Presenter includes a structured presentation for each tutorial of the book, and also gives instructors the flexibility to create custom presentations, complete with matching student notes and lecture notes pages. Instructors can also use Course Presenter to create traditional transparencies.

Course Test Manager: Testing and Practice Online or On Paper   Course Test Manager is cutting-edge Windows-based testing software that helps instructors design and administer pretests, practice tests, and actual examinations. This full-featured program allows students to randomly generate practice tests that provide immediate online feedback and detailed study guides for questions incorrectly answered. Online pretests help instructors assess student skills and plan instruction. Instructors can also use Course Test Manager to produce printed tests. Also, students can take tests at the computer that can be automatically graded and generate statistical information on students' individual and group performance.

Instructor's Manual   Instructor's Manuals are written by the authors. They are available in printed form and through the Course Technology Faculty Online Companion on the World Wide Web. Call your customer service representative for the URL and your password. Each Instructor's Manual contains the following items:

- Instructor's Notes for each tutorial prepared by the authors and based on their teaching experience. Instructor's Notes contain a tutorial overview, tutorial outline, troubleshooting tips, and lecture notes.
- Printed solutions to all of the Tutorial Assignments, Case Problems, and Lab Assignments.
- An Additional Case Problem for each tutorial to augment teaching options.
- Solutions disk(s) containing every file students are asked to create or modify in the Tutorials, Tutorial Assignments, and Case Problems.

Student Files Disks   Student Files Disks contain all of the data files that students will use for the Tutorials, Tutorial Assignments, and Case Problems. A README file includes technical tips for lab management. These files are also available online. See the inside covers of this book and the "Read This Before You Begin" page before Tutorial 1 for more information on student files.

Instructor's Resource Kit   You will receive the following Course Tools in the Instructor's Resource Kit:

- Course Labs Setup Disks
- Course Test Manager Test Bank Disks
- Course Presenter CD-ROM
- Instructor's Manual and Solutions Disks
- Students Files Disks

Acknowledgments

We want to thank all of the New Perspectives Team members for giving us input on essential Windows 95 skills. Their insights and team spirit were invaluable. Many thanks to Joan Carey for her literary contributions and creative input. Thanks to the unequaled technology support we received from Jeff Goding, Jim Valente, Patrick Carey, and Lyle Korytkowski. Our appreciation goes to Catherine Griffin, Debbie Masi, Patty Stephan, and the staff at Gex for their excellent production work. Finally we appreciate the editorial support of Mac Mendelsohn, Kristen Duerr, Barbara Clemens, and Susan Solomon. And still no thanks to Marilyn.

June Parsons
Dan Oja

Brief Contents

Table of **Contents**

TUTORIAL 1

Exploring the Basics

Microsoft
Windows 95

INTRODUCTORY

TUTORIALS

Read This **Before You Begin**

STUDENT DISKS

To complete the Introductory tutorials and Tutorial Assignments you need two Student Disks. Your instructor will either provide you with Student Disks or ask you to make your own.

If you are supposed to make your own Student Disks, you will need two blank, formatted high-density disks. Follow the instructions in the section called "Creating Your Student Disk" in Tutorial 2 to create your Student Disk for Tutorials 1 and 2. Follow the instructions in the section called "Preparing Your Student disk with Quick Format" in Tutorial 3 to create your Student Disk for Tutorials 3 and 4.

The following table shows you which disk you should use with each tutorial:

Student Disk	Write this on the label
1	Student Disk 1: Introductory Tutorials 1-2
2	Student Disk 2: Introductory Tutorials 3-4

When you begin each tutorial, be sure you are using the correct Student Disk. See the inside front or inside back cover of this book for more information on Student Disk files, or ask your instructor or technical support person for assistance.

COURSE LABS

The Introductory tutorials feature four interactive Course Labs to help you understand Windows concepts. There are Lab Assignments at the end of the tutorials that relate to these Labs. To start a Lab, click the **Start** button on the Windows 95 Taskbar, point to **Programs**, point to **CTI Windows 95 Applications**, point to **Windows 95 New Perspective Brief** or **Windows 95 New Perspectives Introductory**, and click the name of the Lab you want to use.

USING YOUR OWN COMPUTER

If you are going to work through this book using your own computer, you need:

- **Computer System** Windows 95 must be installed on your computer. This book assumes a complete installation of Windows 95.

- **Student Disks** Ask your instructor or lab manager for details on how to get the two Student Disks. You will not be able to complete the tutorials or exercises in this book using your own computer until you have the Student Disks. The student files may also be obtained electronically over the Internet. See the inside front or inside back cover of this book for more details.

- **Course Labs** See your instructor or technical support person to obtain the Course Lab software for use on your own computer.

VISIT OUR WORLD WIDE WEB SITE

Additional materials designed especially for you are available on the World Wide Web. Go to **http://coursetools.com**.

To complete the Introductory tutorials and Tutorial Assignments, your students must use a set of files on two Student Disks. The Instructor's Resource Kit CD-ROM for this text contains two setup programs that generate the Student Disks—one in a folder named "Brief" (containing the setup program for Tutorials 1 and 2) and one in a folder named "Introductory" (containing the setup program for Tutorials 3 and 4). To install this software on your server or on standalone computers, follow the instructions in the Readme file.

If you prefer to provide Student Disks rather than letting students generate them, you can run the program that will create Student Disks yourself by following the instructions in Tutorial 2 (for Student Disk 1) and Tutorial 3 (for Student Disk 2).

COURSE LAB SOFTWARE

The Introductory tutorials feature four online, interactive Course Labs that introduce basic Windows concepts. The Instructor's Resource Kit CD-ROM for this text contains two separate Lab installations—one in a folder named "Brief" (which installs the Using a Keyboard, Using a Mouse, and Using Files Labs) and one in a folder named "Introductory" (which installs the Windows Directories, Folders, and Files Lab). To install the Course Lab software, follow the setup instructions in the Readme file on the CD-ROM. Refer also to the Readme file for essential technical notes related to running the labs in a multiuser environment.

Once you have installed the Course Lab software, your students can start the Labs from the Windows 95 desktop by clicking the **Start** button on the Windows 95 taskbar, pointing to **Programs**, pointing to **CTI Windows 95 Applications**, pointing to **Windows 95 New Perspectives Brief** or **Windows 95 New Perspectives Introductory**, and then clicking the name of the Lab they want to use.

CTI COURSE LAB SOFTWARE AND STUDENT FILES

You are granted a license to copy the Student Files and Course Labs to any computer or computer network used by students who have purchased this book.

Exploring the Basics

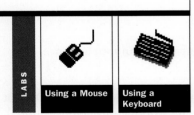

LABS

Using a Mouse **Using a Keyboard**

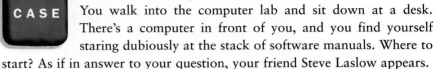

CASE

Your First Day in the Lab

You walk into the computer lab and sit down at a desk. There's a computer in front of you, and you find yourself staring dubiously at the stack of software manuals. Where to start? As if in answer to your question, your friend Steve Laslow appears.

Gesturing to the stack of manuals, you tell Steve that you were just wondering where to start.

"You start with the operating system," says Steve. Noticing your slightly puzzled look, Steve explains that the **operating system** is software that helps the computer carry out basic operating tasks such as displaying information on the computer screen and saving data on your disks. Your computer uses the **Microsoft Windows 95** operating system—Windows 95, for short.

Steve tells you that Windows 95 has a "gooey" or **graphical user interface (GUI)**, which uses pictures of familiar objects, such as file folders and documents, to represent a desktop on your screen. Microsoft Windows 95 gets its name from the rectangular-shaped work areas, called "windows," that appear on your screen.

Steve continues to talk as he sorts through the stack of manuals on your desk. He says there are two things he really likes about Windows 95. First, lots of software is available for computers that have the Windows 95 operating system and all this software has a standard graphical user interface. That means once you have learned how to use one Windows software package, such as word-processing software, you are well on your way to understanding how to use other Windows software. Second, Windows 95 lets you use more than one software package at a time, so you can easily switch between your word-processing software and your appointment book software, for example. All in all, Windows 95 makes your computer an effective and easy-to-use productivity tool.

Steve recommends that you get started right away by using some tutorials that will teach you the skills essential for using Microsoft Windows 95. He hands you a book and assures you that everything on your computer system is set up and ready to go.

You mention that last summer you worked in an advertising agency where the employees used something called Windows 3.1. Steve explains that Windows 3.1 is an earlier version of the Windows operating system. Windows 95 and Windows 3.1 are similar, but Windows 95 is more powerful and easier to use. Steve says that as you work through the tutorials you will see notes that point out the important differences between Windows 95 and Windows 3.1.

Steve has a class, but he says he'll check back later to see how you are doing.

Using the Tutorials Effectively

These tutorials will help you learn about Windows 95. The tutorials are designed to be used at a computer. Each tutorial is divided into sessions. Watch for the session headings, such as Session 1.1 and Session 1.2. Each session is designed to be completed in about 45 minutes, but take as much time as you need. It's also a good idea to take a break between sessions.

Before you begin, read the following questions and answers. They are designed to help you use the tutorials effectively.

Where do I start?

Each tutorial begins with a case, which sets the scene for the tutorial and gives you background information to help you understand what you will be doing in the tutorial. Read the case before you go to the lab. In the lab, begin with the first session of the tutorial.

How do I know what to do on the computer?

Each session contains steps that you will perform on the computer to learn how to use Windows 95. Read the text that introduces each series of steps. The steps you need to do at a computer are numbered and are set against a color background. Read each step carefully and completely before you try it.

How do I know if I did the step correctly?

As you work, compare your computer screen with the corresponding figure in the tutorial. Don't worry if your screen display is somewhat different from the figure. The important parts of the screen display are labeled in each figure. Check to make sure these parts are on your screen.

What if I make a mistake?

Don't worry about making mistakes—they are part of the learning process. Paragraphs labeled "TROUBLE?" identify common problems and explain how to get back on track. Follow the steps in a TROUBLE? paragraph *only* if you are having the problem described. If you run into other problems:

- Carefully consider the current state of your system, the position of the pointer, and any messages on the screen.

- Complete the sentence, "Now I want to...." Be specific, because you are identifying your goal.

- Develop a plan for accomplishing your goal, and put your plan into action.

How do I use the Reference Windows?

Reference Windows summarize the procedures you learn in the tutorial steps. Do not complete the actions in the Reference Windows when you are working through the tutorial. Instead, refer to the Reference Windows while you are working on the assignments at the end of the tutorial.

How can I test my understanding of the material I learned in the tutorial?

At the end of each session, you can answer the Quick Check questions. The answers for the Quick Checks are at the end of the book.

After you have completed the entire tutorial, you should complete the Tutorial Assignments. The Tutorial Assignments are carefully structured so you will review what you have learned and then apply your knowledge to new situations.

What if I can't remember how to do something?

You should refer to the Task Reference at the end of the book; it summarizes how to accomplish commonly performed tasks.

What are the 3.1 Notes?

The 3.1 Notes are helpful if you have used Windows 3.1. The notes point out the key similarities and differences between Windows 3.1 and Windows 95.

What are the Interactive Labs, and how should I use them?

Interactive Labs help you review concepts and practice skills that you learn in the tutorial. Lab icons at the beginning of each tutorial and in the margins of the tutorials indicate topics that have corresponding Labs. The Lab Assignments section includes instructions for how to use each Lab.

Now that you understand how to use the tutorials effectively, you are ready to begin.

SESSION

1.1

In this session, in addition to learning basic Windows terminology, you will learn how to use a mouse, to start and stop a program, and to use more than one program at a time. With the skills you learn in this session, you will be able to use Windows 95 to start software programs.

Using a Keyboard

Starting Windows 95

Windows 95 automatically starts when you turn on the computer. Depending on the way your computer is set up, you might be asked to enter your user name and password. If prompted to do so, type your assigned user name and press the Enter key. Then type your password and press the Enter key to continue.

To start Windows 95:

> **1.** Turn on your computer.

The Windows 95 Desktop

In Windows terminology, the screen represents a **desktop**—a workspace for projects and the tools needed to manipulate those projects. Look at your screen display and locate the objects labeled in Figure 1-1 on the following page.

Because it is easy to customize the Windows environment, your screen might not look exactly the same as Figure 1-1. You should, however, be able to locate objects on your screen similar to those in Figure 1-1.

TROUBLE? If the Welcome to Windows 95 box appears on your screen, press the Enter key to close it.

Icons are small pictures that represent objects such as your computer, your computer network, a specific computer program, or a document. Your desktop probably contains several icons, such as My Computer, Network Neighborhood, and the Recycle Bin. You'll use these icons in later tutorials to work with files stored on your computer or on other computers on the network.

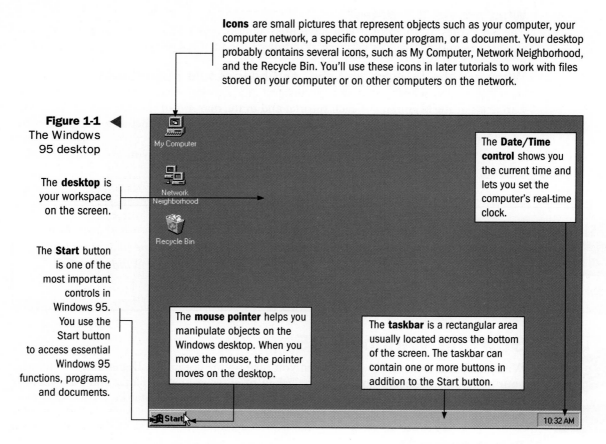

Figure 1-1 ◀
The Windows 95 desktop

The **desktop** is your workspace on the screen.

The **Start** button is one of the most important controls in Windows 95. You use the Start button to access essential Windows 95 functions, programs, and documents.

The **Date/Time control** shows you the current time and lets you set the computer's real-time clock.

The **mouse pointer** helps you manipulate objects on the Windows desktop. When you move the mouse, the pointer moves on the desktop.

The **taskbar** is a rectangular area usually located across the bottom of the screen. The taskbar can contain one or more buttons in addition to the Start button.

My Computer

Network Neighborhood

Recycle Bin

Start   10:32 AM

TROUBLE? If the screen goes blank or starts to display a moving design, press any key to restore the image.

Using the Mouse

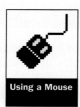

Using a Mouse

A **mouse,** like those shown in Figure 1-2, is a pointing device that helps you interact with objects on the screen. In Windows 95 you need to know how to use the mouse to point, click, and drag. In this session you will learn about pointing and clicking. In Session 1.2 you will learn how to use the mouse to drag objects.

You can also interact with objects by using the keyboard; however, the mouse is much more convenient for most tasks, so the tutorials in this book assume you are using one.

Pointing

The **pointer,** or **mouse pointer,** is a small object that moves on the screen when you move the mouse. The pointer is usually shaped like an arrow. As you move the mouse on a flat surface, the pointer on the screen moves in the direction corresponding to the movement of the mouse. The pointer sometimes changes shape depending on where it is on the screen or the action the computer is completing.

Find the arrow-shaped pointer on your screen. If you do not see the pointer, move your mouse until the pointer comes into view.

Figure 1-2 ◀
The mouse

A two-button mouse is the standard mouse configuration for computers that run Windows.

A three-button mouse features a left, right, and center button. The center button might be set up to send a double-click signal to the computer even when you only press it once.

To hold the mouse, place your forefinger over the left mouse button. Place your thumb on the left side of the mouse. Your ring and small fingers should be on the right side of the mouse.

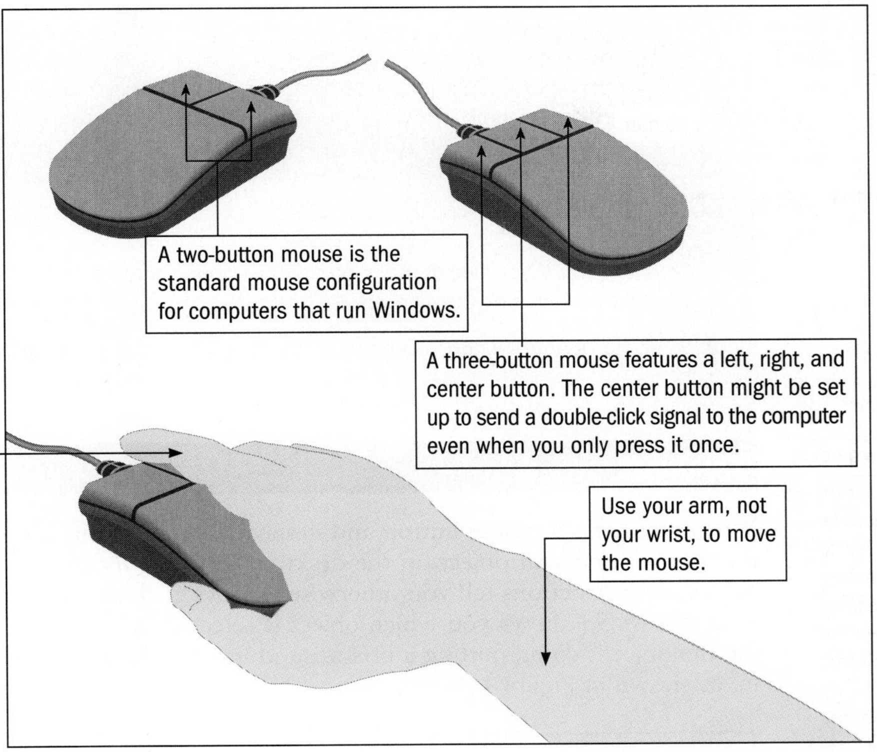

Use your arm, not your wrist, to move the mouse.

Basic "mousing" skills depend on your ability to position the pointer. You begin most Windows operations by positioning the pointer over a specific part of the screen. This is called **pointing**.

To move the pointer:

1. Position your right index finger over the left mouse button, as shown in Figure 1-2. Lightly grasp the sides of the mouse with your thumb and little finger.

   TROUBLE? If you want to use the mouse with your left hand, ask your instructor or technical support person to help you use the Control Panel to change the mouse settings to swap the left and right mouse buttons. Be sure you find out how to change back to the right-handed mouse setting, so you can reset the mouse each time you are finished in the lab.

2. Locate the arrow-shaped pointer on the screen.

3. Move the mouse and watch the movement of the pointer.

If you run out of room to move your mouse, lift the mouse and move it to a clear area on your desk, then place the mouse back on the desk. Notice that the pointer does not move when the mouse is not in contact with the desk.

When you position the mouse pointer over certain objects, such as the objects on the taskbar, a "tip" appears. These "tips" are called **ToolTips**, and they tell you the purpose or function of an object.

To view ToolTips:

1. Use the mouse to point to the **Start** button ⊞Start. After a few seconds, you see the tip "Click here to begin" as shown in Figure 1-3 on the following page.

Figure 1-3 ◀
Viewing ToolTips

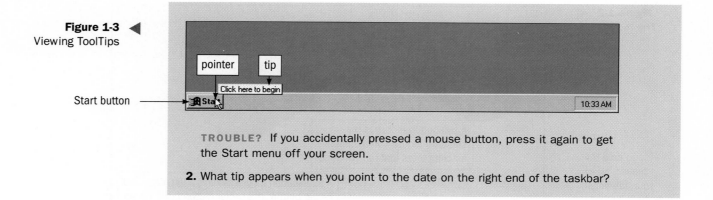

Start button —

TROUBLE? If you accidentally pressed a mouse button, press it again to get the Start menu off your screen.

2. What tip appears when you point to the date on the right end of the taskbar?

Clicking

When you press a mouse button and immediately release it, it is called **clicking**. Clicking the mouse selects an object on the desktop. *You usually click the left mouse button, so unless the instructions tell you otherwise, always click the left mouse button.*

Windows 95 shows you which object is selected by highlighting it, usually by changing the object's color, putting a box around it, or making the object appear to be pushed in, as shown in Figure 1-4.

Figure 1-4 ◀
Selected objects

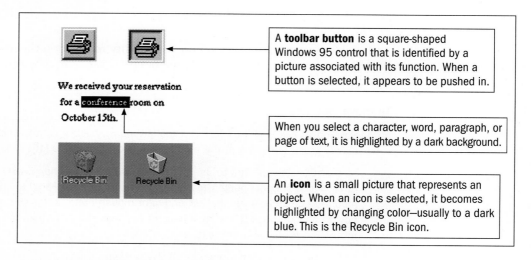

A **toolbar button** is a square-shaped Windows 95 control that is identified by a picture associated with its function. When a button is selected, it appears to be pushed in.

When you select a character, word, paragraph, or page of text, it is highlighted by a dark background.

An **icon** is a small picture that represents an object. When an icon is selected, it becomes highlighted by changing color—usually to a dark blue. This is the Recycle Bin icon.

To select the Recycle Bin icon:

1. Position the pointer over the **Recycle Bin** icon.

2. Click the mouse button and notice how the color of the icon changes to show that it is selected.

Starting and Closing a Program

The software you use is sometimes referred to as a program or an application. To use a program, such as a word-processing program, you must first start it. With Windows 95 you start a program by clicking the Start button. The Start button displays a menu.

A **menu** is a list of options. Windows 95 has a **Start menu** that provides you with access to programs, data, and configuration options. One of the Start menu's most important functions is to let you start a program.

The Reference Window below explains how to start a program. Don't do the steps in the Reference Window now; they are for your later reference.

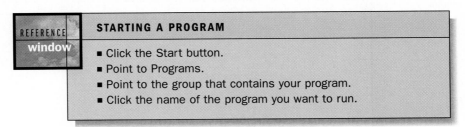

REFERENCE window	**STARTING A PROGRAM**
	■ Click the Start button.
	■ Point to Programs.
	■ Point to the group that contains your program.
	■ Click the name of the program you want to run.

3.1 NOTE

WordPad is similar to Write in Windows 3.1.

Windows 95 includes an easy-to-use word-processing program called WordPad. Suppose you want to start the WordPad program and use it to write a letter or report.

To start the WordPad program from the Start menu:

1. Click the **Start** button ⊞**Start** as shown in Figure 1-5. A menu appears.

Figure 1-5 ◀
Starting the
WordPad program

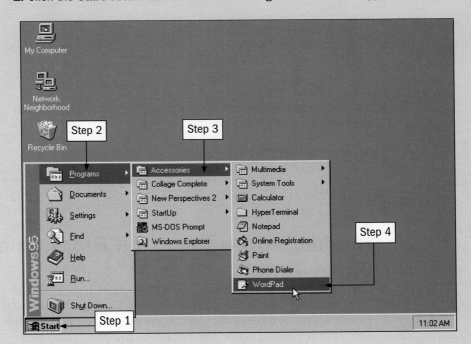

2. Point to **Programs**. After a short pause, the next menu appears.

TROUBLE? If you don't get the correct menu, go back and point to the correct menu option.

3. Point to **Accessories**. Another menu appears.

4. Click **WordPad**. Make sure you can see the WordPad program as shown in Figure 1-6 on the following page.

Figure 1-6 ◀
The WordPad
program

WordPad program
window

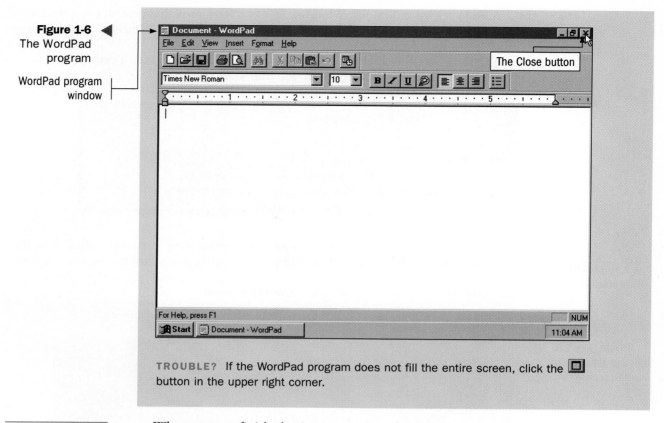

TROUBLE? If the WordPad program does not fill the entire screen, click the 🔲 button in the upper right corner.

3.1 NOTE

As with Windows 3.1, in Windows 95 you can also exit a program using the Exit option from the File menu.

When you are finished using a program, the easiest way to return to the Windows 95 desktop is to click the Close button ✗.

To exit the WordPad program:

1. Click the **Close** button ✗. See Figure 1-6. You will be returned to the Windows 95 desktop.

Running More than One Program at the Same Time

3.1 NOTE

Paint in Windows 95 is similar to Paintbrush in Windows 3.1.

One of the most useful features of Windows 95 is its ability to run multiple programs at the same time. This feature, known as **multi-tasking**, allows you to work on more than one task at a time and to quickly switch between tasks. For example, you can start WordPad and leave it running while you then start the Paint program.

To run WordPad and Paint at the same time:

1. Start WordPad.

   TROUBLE? You learned how to start WordPad earlier in the tutorial: Click the Start button, point to Programs, point to Accessories, and then click WordPad.

2. Now you can start the Paint program. Click the **Start** button 🏁Start again.

3. Point to **Programs**.

4. Point to **Accessories**.

5. Click **Paint**. The Paint program appears as shown in Figure 1-7. Now two programs are running at the same time.

TROUBLE? If the Paint program does not fill the entire screen, click the 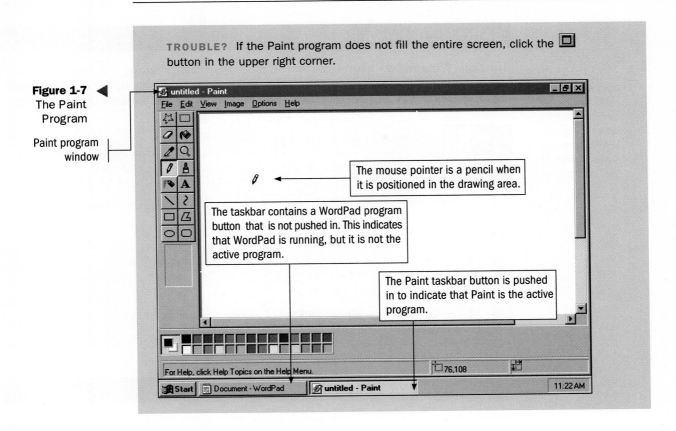 button in the upper right corner.

Figure 1-7 ◀
The Paint
Program

Paint program
window

What happened to WordPad? The WordPad button is still on the taskbar, so even if you can't see it, WordPad is still running. You can imagine that it is stacked behind the Paint program, as shown in Figure 1-8.

3.1 NOTE

With Windows 3.1, some users had difficulty finding program windows on the desktop. The buttons on the Windows 95 taskbar make it much easier to keep track of which programs are running.

Figure 1-8 ◀
Programs
stacked on top
of a desk

Think of your screen as the main work area of your desk.

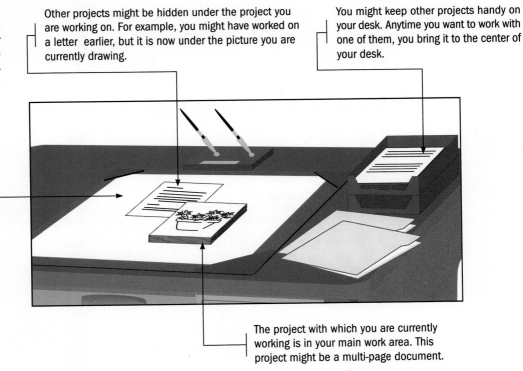

Other projects might be hidden under the project you are working on. For example, you might have worked on a letter earlier, but it is now under the picture you are currently drawing.

You might keep other projects handy on your desk. Anytime you want to work with one of them, you bring it to the center of your desk.

The project with which you are currently working is in your main work area. This project might be a multi-page document.

Switching Between Programs

Although Windows 95 allows you to run more than one program, only one program at a time is active. The **active** program is the program with which you are currently working. The easiest way to switch between programs is to use the buttons on the taskbar.

REFERENCE window	SWITCHING BETWEEN PROGRAMS
	▪ Click the taskbar button that contains the name of the program to which you want to switch.

To switch between WordPad and Paint:

1. Click the button labeled **Document - WordPad** on the taskbar. The Document - WordPad button now looks like it has been pushed in to indicate it is the active program.

2. Next, click the button labeled **untitled - Paint** on the taskbar to switch to the Paint program.

Closing WordPad and Paint

It is good practice to close each program when you are finished using it. Each program uses computer resources such as memory, so Windows 95 works more efficiently when only the programs you need are open.

To close WordPad and Paint:

1. Click the **Close** button ☒ for the Paint program. The button labeled "untitled - Paint" disappears from the taskbar.

2. Click the **Close** button ☒ for the WordPad program. The WordPad button disappears from the taskbar, and you return to the Windows 95 desktop.

Shutting Down Windows 95

It is very important to shut down Windows 95 before you turn off the computer. If you turn off your computer without correctly shutting down, you might lose data and damage your files.

To shut down Windows 95:

1. Click the **Start** button 🏁 Start on the taskbar to display the Start menu.

2. Click the **Shut Down** menu option to display the Shut Down Windows options screen.

3. Make sure the **Shut down the computer?** option is selected.

4. Click the **Yes** button.

5. Wait until you see a message indicating it is safe to turn off your computer, then switch off your computer.

You should typically use the option "Shut down the computer?" when you want to turn off your computer. However, other shut-down options are available. For example, your school might prefer that you select the option to "Close all programs and log on as a different user." This option logs you out of Windows 95, leaves the computer turned on, and allows another user to log on without restarting the computer. Check with your instructor or technical support person for the preferred method for your school's computer lab.

Quick Check

1 Label the components of the Windows 95 desktop in the figure below:

Figure 1-9 ◀

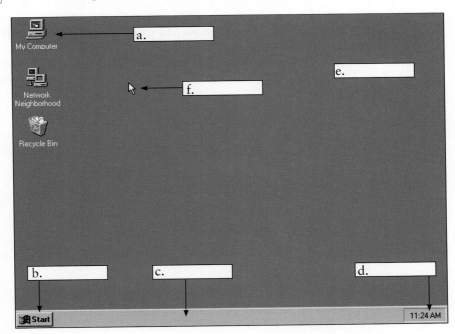

2 The _____ feature of Windows 95 allows you to run more than one program at a time.

3 The _____ is a list of options that provides you with access to programs, data, and configuration options.

4 What should you do if you are trying to move the pointer to the left edge of your screen, but your mouse runs into the keyboard?

5 Windows 95 shows you that an icon is selected by _____ it.

6 Even if you can't see a program, it might be running. How can you tell if a program is running?

7 Why is it good practice to close each program when you are finished using it?

8 Why do you need to shut down Windows 95 before you turn off your computer?

SESSION

1.2

In this session you will learn how to use many of the Windows 95 controls to manipulate windows and programs. You will learn how to change the size and shape of a window and to move a window so that you can customize your screen-based workspace. You will also learn how to use menus, dialog boxes, tabs, buttons, and lists to specify how you want a program to carry out a task.

Anatomy of a Window

When you run a program in Windows 95, it appears in a window. A **window** is a rectangular area of the screen that contains a program or data. A window also contains controls for manipulating the window and using the program. WordPad is a good example of how a window works.

Windows, spelled with an uppercase "W," is the name of the Microsoft operating system. The word "window" with a lowercase "w" refers to one of the rectangular windows on the screen.

To look at window controls:

1. Make sure Windows 95 is running and you are at the Windows 95 desktop screen.

2. Start WordPad.

   TROUBLE? To start WordPad, click the **Start** button, point to Programs, point to Accessories, and then click **WordPad**.

3. Make sure WordPad takes up the entire screen.

   TROUBLE? If WordPad does not take up the entire screen, click the 🔲 button in the upper right corner.

4. On your screen, identify the controls labeled in Figure 1-10.

Figure 1-10 ◀
Window
controls

The **menu bar** contains the titles of menus, such as File, Edit, and Help.

The **toolbar** contains buttons that provide you with a shortcut to the commands listed on the menus.

The **status bar** provides you with abbreviated help relevant to the task you are doing.

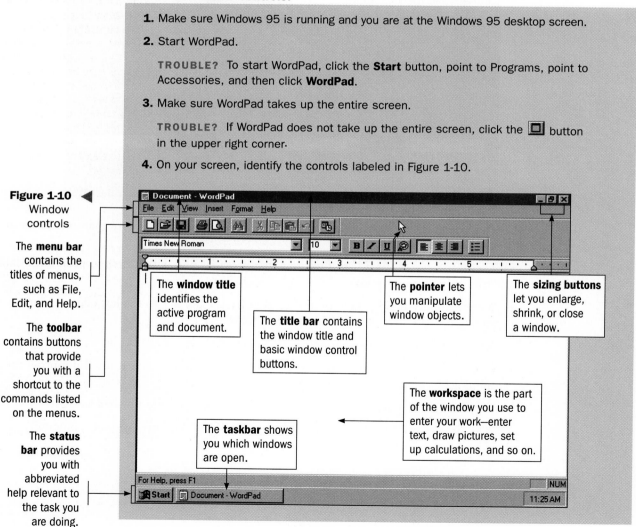

The **window title** identifies the active program and document.

The **title bar** contains the window title and basic window control buttons.

The **pointer** lets you manipulate window objects.

The **sizing buttons** let you enlarge, shrink, or close a window.

The **workspace** is the part of the window you use to enter your work—enter text, draw pictures, set up calculations, and so on.

The **taskbar** shows you which windows are open.

Manipulating a Window

There are three buttons located on the right side of the title bar. You are already familiar with the Close button. The Minimize button hides the window. The other button either maximizes the window or restores it to a predefined size. Figure 1-11 shows how these buttons work.

Figure 1-11 ◀
Minimize,
Maximize and
Restore buttons

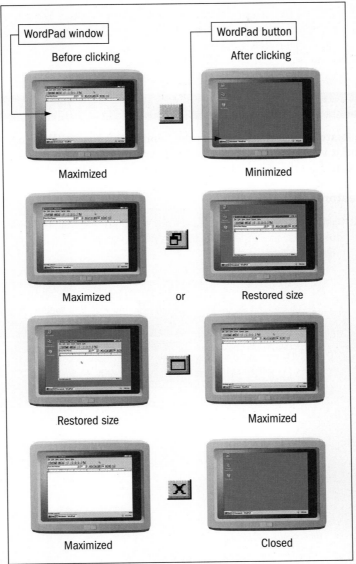

The **Minimize button** 🗕 shrinks the window, so you only see its button on the taskbar.

The middle button appears as a **Restore button** 🗗 or a **Maximize button.** 🗖 When the window is maximized, the Restore button appears. It can be used to reduce the size of the window to a predetermined or "normal" size. When the window does not fill the entire screen, the Maximize button appears. Clicking the Maximize button enlarges the window to fill the screen.

The **Close button** 🗙 closes the window and removes its button from the taskbar at the bottom of the screen.

Minimizing a Window

The **Minimize button** 🗕 shrinks the current window so that only the button on the taskbar remains visible. You can use the Minimize button when you want to temporarily hide a window but keep the program running.

To minimize the WordPad window:

1. Click the **Minimize** button 🗕. The WordPad window shrinks so only the Document - WordPad button on the taskbar is visible.

TROUBLE? If you accidentally clicked the Close button and closed the window, use the Start button to start WordPad again.

Redisplaying a Window

You can redisplay a minimized window by clicking the program's button on the taskbar. When you redisplay a window, it becomes the active window.

To redisplay the WordPad window:

1. Click the **Document - WordPad** button on the taskbar. The WordPad window is restored to its previous size. The Document - WordPad button looks pushed in as a visual clue that it is now the active window.

Restoring a Window

The **Restore** button 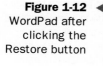 reduces the window so it is smaller than the entire screen. This is useful if you want to see more than one window at a time. Also, because of its small size, you can drag the window to another location on the screen or change its dimensions.

To restore a window:

1. Click the **Restore** button on the WordPad title bar. The WordPad window will look similar to Figure 1-12, but the exact size of the window on your screen might be slightly different.

Figure 1-12
WordPad after clicking the Restore button

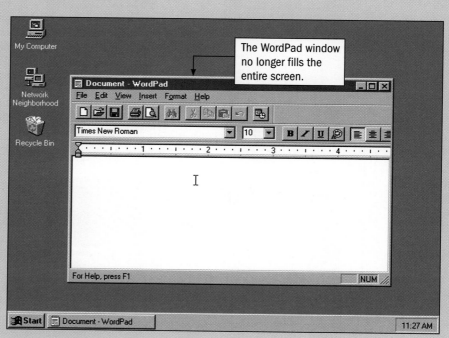

Moving a Window

You can use the mouse to **move** a window to a new position on the screen. When you hold down the mouse button while moving the mouse, it is called **dragging**. You can move objects on the screen by dragging them to a new location. If you want to move a window, you drag its title bar.

To drag the WordPad window to a new location:

1. Position the mouse pointer on the WordPad window title bar.

2. While you hold down the left mouse button, move the mouse to drag the window. A rectangle representing the window moves as you move the mouse.

3. Position the rectangle anywhere on the screen, then release the left mouse button. The WordPad window appears in the new location.

4. Now drag the WordPad window to the upper-left corner of the screen.

Changing the Size of a Window

You can also use the mouse to change the size of a window. Notice the sizing handle at the lower right corner of the window. The **sizing handle** provides a visible control for changing the size of a current window.

To change the size of the WordPad window:

1. Position the pointer over the sizing handle . The pointer changes to a diagonal arrow .

2. While holding down the mouse button, drag the sizing handle down and to the right.

3. Release the mouse button. Now the window is larger.

4. Practice using the sizing handle to make the WordPad window larger or smaller.

Maximizing a Window

The **Maximize button** enlarges a window so that it fills the entire screen. You will probably do most of your work using maximized windows because you can see more of your program and data.

To maximize the WordPad window:

1. Click the **Maximize** button on the WordPad title bar.

Using Program Menus

Most Windows programs use menus to provide an easy way for you to select program commands. The **menu bar** is typically located at the top of the program window and shows the titles of menus such as File, Edit, and Help.

Windows menus are relatively standardized—most Windows programs include similar menu options. It's easy to learn new programs, because you can make a pretty good guess about which menu contains the command you want.

Selecting Commands from a Menu

When you click any menu title, choices for that menu appear below the menu bar. These choices are referred to as **menu options**. To select a menu option, you click it. For example, the File menu is a standard feature in most Windows programs and contains the options related to working with a file: creating, opening, saving, and printing a file or document.

To select Print Preview from the File menu:

1. Click **File** in the WordPad menu bar to display the File menu.

    TROUBLE? If you open a menu but decide not to select any of the menu options, you can close the menu by clicking its title again.

2. Click **Print Preview** to open the preview screen and view your document as it will appear when printed. This document is blank because you didn't enter any text.

3. After examining the screen, click the button labeled "Close" to return to your document.

Not all menu options immediately carry out an action—some show submenus or ask you for more information about what you want to do. The menu gives you hints about what to expect when you select an option. These hints are sometimes referred to as **menu conventions.** Study Figures 1-13a and 1-13b so you will recognize the Windows 95 menu conventions.

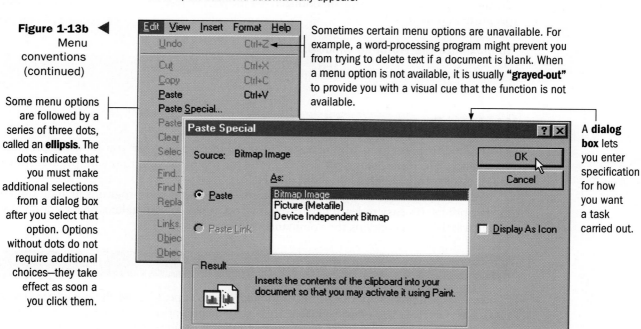

Figure 1-13a
Menu Conventions

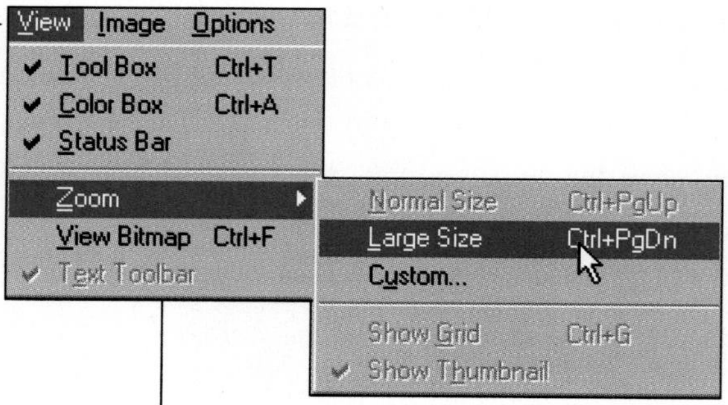

Some menu options are toggle switches that can be either "on" or "off." When a feature is turned on, **a check mark** appears next to the menu option. When the feature is turned off, there is no check mark.

Certain menu selections lead you to an additional menu, called a **submenu.** A triangle on the right side of the menu choice indicates menu options that lead to submenus. When you move the pointer to a menu option with a triangle next to it, the submenu automatically appears.

Figure 1-13b
Menu conventions (continued)

Some menu options are followed by a series of three dots, called an **ellipsis**. The dots indicate that you must make additional selections from a dialog box after you select that option. Options without dots do not require additional choices—they take effect as soon a you click them.

Sometimes certain menu options are unavailable. For example, a word-processing program might prevent you from trying to delete text if a document is blank. When a menu option is not available, it is usually **"grayed-out"** to provide you with a visual cue that the function is not available.

A **dialog box** lets you enter specification for how you want a task carried out.

Using Toolbars

A **toolbar** contains buttons that provide quick access to important program commands. Although you can usually perform all program commands using the menus, the toolbar provides convenient one-click access to frequently-used commands. For most Windows 95 functions, there is usually more than one way to accomplish a task. To simplify your introduction to Windows 95 in this tutorial, you will learn only one method for performing a task. As you become more accomplished using Windows 95, you can explore alternative methods.

In Session 1.1 you learned that Windows 95 programs include ToolTips that indicate the purpose and function of a tool. Now is a good time to explore the WordPad toolbar buttons by looking at their ToolTips.

To find out a toolbar button's function:

1. Position the pointer over any button on the toolbar, such as the Print Preview icon. After a short pause, the name of the button appears in a box and a description of the button appears in the status bar just above the Start button.

2. Move the pointer to each button on the toolbar to see its name and purpose.

You select a toolbar button by clicking it.

To select the Print Preview toolbar button:

1. Click the **Print Preview** button.

2. The Print Preview dialog box appears. This is the same dialog box that appeared when you selected File, Print Preview from the menu bar.

3. Click ⬚Close⬚ to close the Print Preview dialog box.

Using List Boxes and Scroll Bars

As you might guess from the name, a **list box** displays a list of choices. In WordPad, date and time formats are shown in the Date/Time list box. List box controls include arrow buttons, a scroll bar, and a scroll box, as shown in Figure 1-14.

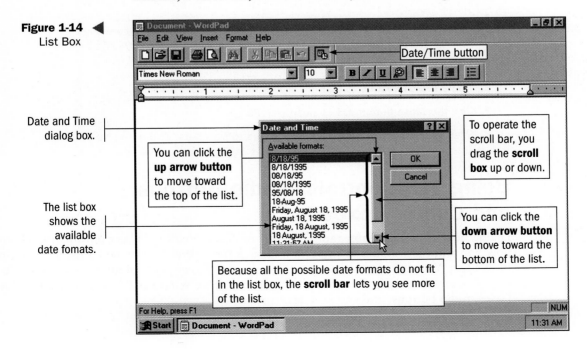

Figure 1-14 ◄
List Box

Date and Time dialog box.

You can click the **up arrow button** to move toward the top of the list.

The list box shows the available date fomats.

To operate the scroll bar, you drag the **scroll box** up or down.

You can click the **down arrow button** to move toward the bottom of the list.

Because all the possible date formats do not fit in the list box, the **scroll bar** lets you see more of the list.

To use the Date/Time list box:

1. Click the **Date/Time** button 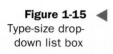 to display the Date and Time dialog box. See Figure 1-14.

2. To scroll down the list, click the **down arrow** button ▼. See Figure 1-14.

3. Find the scroll box on your screen. See Figure 1-14.

4. Drag the **scroll box** to the top of the scroll bar. Notice how the list scrolls back to the beginning.

5. Find a date format similar to "October 2, 1997." Click that date format to select it.

6. Click the **OK** button to close the Date and Time list box. This inserts the current date in your document.

A variation of the list box, called a **drop-down list box**, usually shows only one choice, but can expand down to display additional choices on the list.

To use the Type Size drop-down list:

1. Click the **down arrow** button ▼ shown in Figure 1-15.

Figure 1-15 ◀
Type-size drop-down list box

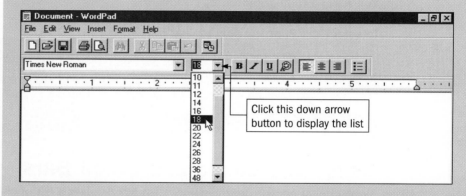

2. Click **18**. The drop-down list disappears and the type size you selected appears at the top of the pull-down list.

3. Type a few characters to test the new type size.

4. Click the **down arrow** button ▼ in the Type size drop-down list box again.

5. Click **12**.

6. Type a few characters to test this type size.

7. Click the **Close** button ✕ to close WordPad.

8. When you see the message "Save changes to Document?" click the **No** button.

Using Tab Controls, Radio Buttons, and Check Boxes

Dialog boxes often use tabs, radio buttons, or check boxes to collect information about how you want a program to perform a task. A **tab control** is patterned after the tabs on file folders. You click the appropriate tab to view different pages of information or choices. Tab controls are often used as containers for other Windows 95 controls such as list boxes, radio buttons, and check boxes.

Radio buttons, also called **option buttons**, allow you to select a single option from among one or more options. **Check boxes** allow you to select many options at the same time. Figure 1-16 explains how to use these controls.

Figure 1-16 ◀
Tabs, radio buttons, and check boxes

A **tab** indicates an "index card" that contains information or a group of controls, usually with related functions. To look at the functions on an index card, click the tab.

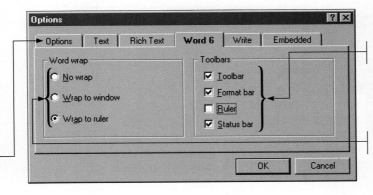

Check boxes allow you to select one or more options from a group. When you click a check box, a check mark appears in it. To remove a check mark from a box, click it again.

Radio buttons are round and usually come in groups of two or more. You can select only one radio button from a group. Your selection is indicated by a black dot.

Using Help

Windows 95 **Help** provides on-screen information about the program you are using. Help for the Windows 95 operating system is available by clicking the Start button on the taskbar, then selecting Help from the Start menu. If you want Help for a program, such as WordPad, you must first start the program, then use the Help menu at the top of the screen.

REFERENCE
window

STARTING WINDOWS 95 HELP

■ Click the Start button.
■ Click Help.

To start Windows 95 Help:

1. Click the **Start** button.

2. Click **Help**.

Help uses tabs for each section of Help. Windows 95 Help tabs include Contents, Index, and Find as shown in Figure 1-17 on the following page.

Figure 1-17 ◄
Windows 95
Help

Each section of
Help is divided
into "books."
To open a book,
you click the
book, then click
the Open button.

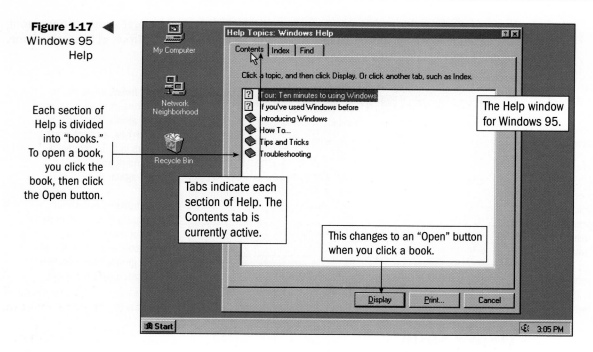

The Contents **tab** groups Help topics into a series of books. You select a book, which then provides you with a list of related topics from which you can choose. The **Index tab** displays an alphabetical list of all the Help topics from which you can choose. The **Find tab** lets you search for any word or phrase in Help.

Suppose you're wondering if there is an alternative way to start programs. You can use the Contents tab to find the answer to your question.

3.1 NOTE

You can also double-click to select and open a topic in a single step.

To use the Contents tab:

1. Click the **Contents** tab to display the Contents window.

2. Click the **How To...** book title, then click the **Open** button. A list of related books appears below the book title. See. Figure 1-18.

Figure 1-18 ◄
Help Window

Click this book,
then click the
Open button to
display a list of
related books.

Books related to
the "How To" topic.

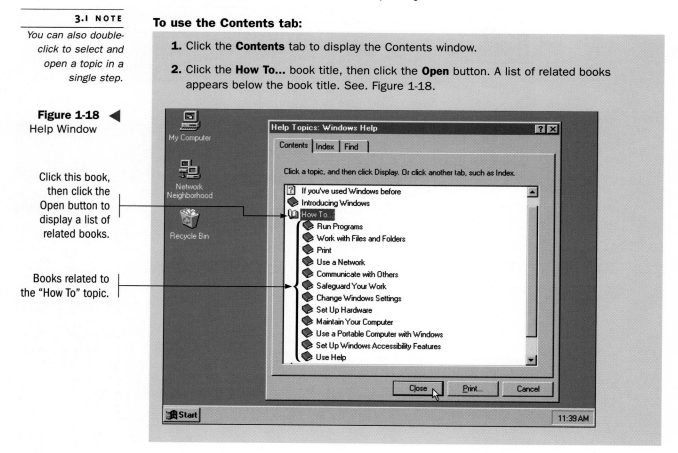

3. Click the **Run Programs** book, then click the **Open** button. The table of contents for this Help book is displayed.

4. Click the topic **Starting a Program**, then click the **Display** button. A Help window appears and explains how to start a program.

Help also provides you with definitions of technical terms. You can click any underlined term to see its definition.

To see a definition of the term "taskbar":

1. Point to the underlined term, **taskbar** until the pointer changes to a hand. Then click.

2. After you have read the definition, click the definition to deselect it.

3. Click the **Close** button ☒ on the Help window.

The **Index tab** allows you to jump to a Help topic by selecting a topic from an indexed list. For example, you can use the Index tab to learn how to arrange the open windows on your desktop.

To find a Help topic using the Index tab:

1. Click the **Start** button.

2. Click **Help**.

3. Click the **Index** tab.

4. A long list of indexed Help topics appears. Drag the scroll box down to view additional topics.

5. You can quickly jump to any part of the list by typing the first few characters of a word or phrase in the line above the Index list. Type **desktop** to display topics related to the Windows 95 desktop.

6. Click the topic **arranging open windows on** in the bottom window.

7. Click the **Display** button as shown in Figure 1-19.

Figure 1-19 ◄
Displaying a
Help Topic

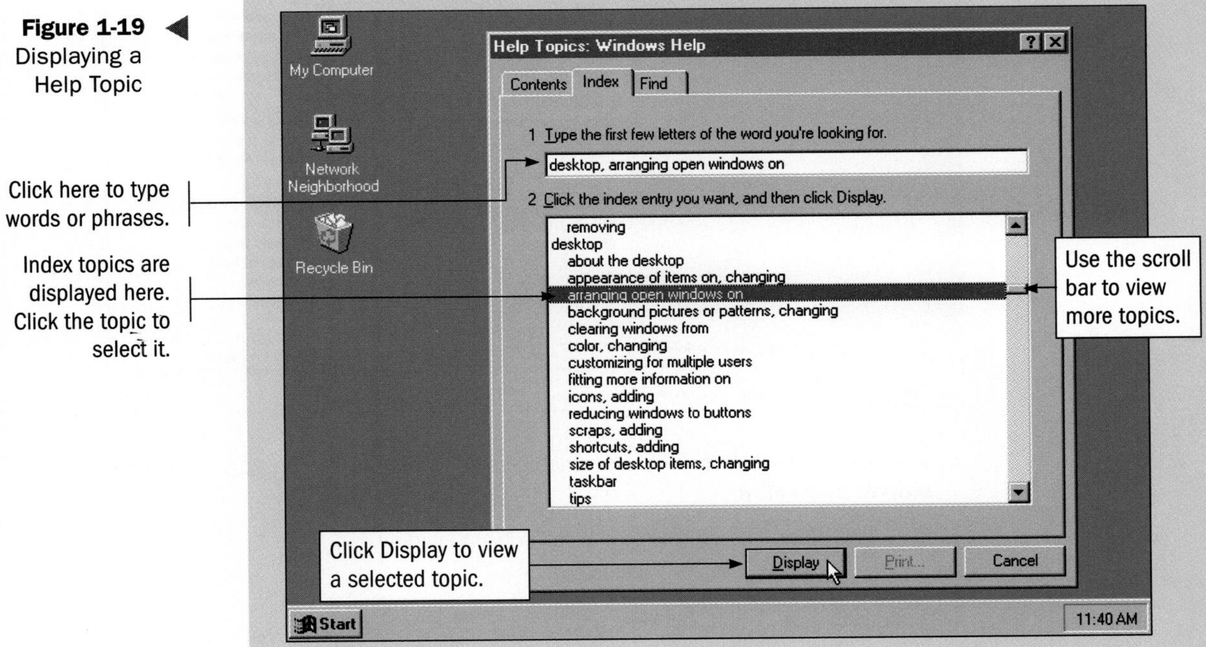

Click here to type
words or phrases.

Index topics are
displayed here.
Click the topic to
select it.

Use the scroll
bar to view
more topics.

Click Display to view
a selected topic.

8. Click the **Close** button ⊠ to close the Windows Help window.

The **Find tab** contains an index of all words in Windows 95 Help. You can use it to search for Help pages that contain a particular word or phrase. For example, suppose you heard that a screen saver blanks out your screen when you are not using it. You could use the Find tab to find out more about screen savers.

To find a Help topic using the Find tab:

1. Click the **Start** button 🎇 Start.

2. Click **Help**.

3. Click the **Find** tab.

TROUBLE? If the Find index has not yet been created on your computer, the computer will prompt you through several steps to create the index. Continue with Step 4 below after the Find index is created.

4. Type **screen** to display a list of all topics that start with the letters "screen."

5. Click **screen-saver** in the middle window to display the topics that contain the word "screen-saver."

6. Click **Having your monitor automatically turn off**, then click the **Display** button.

7. Click the **Help window** button shown in Figure 1-20. The screen saver is shown on a simulated monitor.

TROUBLE? If you see an error message, your lab does not allow students to modify screen savers. Click the OK button and go to Step 9.

Figure 1-20 ◀
Clicking a
Button in Help

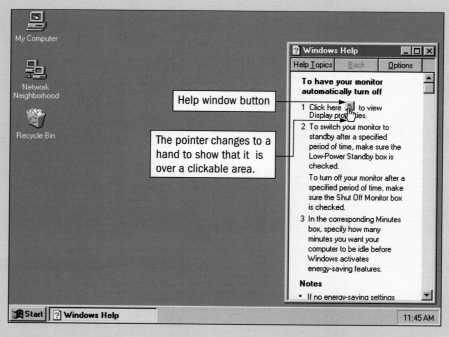

8. To close the Display properties window, click the **Close** button ⊠ in the Display Properties window.

9. Click the **Close** button ⊠ to close the Help window.

Now that you know how Windows 95 Help works, don't forget to use it! Use Help when you need to perform a new task or when you forget how to complete a procedure.

Quick Check

1 Label the parts of the window shown in Figure 1-21.

Figure 1-21 ◄

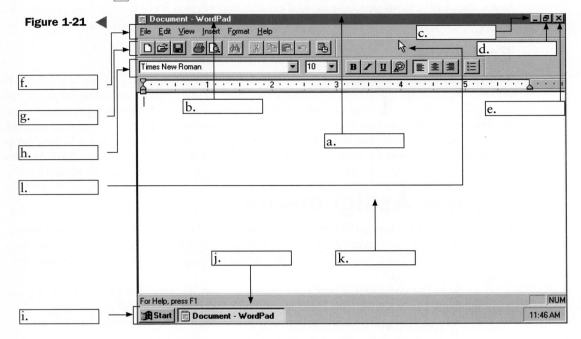

f.
g.
h.
l.
i.

b.
a.
c.
d.
e.
j.
k.

2 Provide the name and purpose of each button:
a.
b.
c.
d.

3 Explain each of the following menu conventions:
a. Ellipsis...
b. Grayed out
c. ▶
d. ✔

4 A(n) _____ consists of a group of buttons, each of which provides one-click access to important program functions.

5 Label each part of the dialog box below:

Figure 1-22 ◄

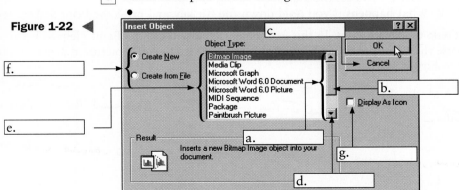

f.
e.
c.
a.
d.
b.
g.

6. Radio buttons allow you to select _____ option(s) at a time, but _____ allow you to select one or more options.

7. It is a good idea to use _____ when you need to learn how to perform new tasks, simplify tedious procedures, and correct actions that did not turn out as you expected.

End Note

You've finished the tutorial, but Steve Laslow still hasn't returned. Take a moment to review what you have learned. You now know how to start a program using the Start button. You can run more than one program at a time and switch between programs using the buttons on the taskbar. You have learned the names and functions of window controls and Windows 95 menu conventions. You can now use toolbar buttons, list boxes, drop-down lists, radio buttons, check boxes, and scroll bars. Finally, you can use the Contents, Index, and Find tabs in Help to extend your knowledge of how to use Windows 95.

Tutorial Assignments

1. Running Two Programs and Switching Between Them In this tutorial you learned how to run more than one program at a time using WordPad and Paint. You can run other programs at the same time, too. Complete the following steps and write out your answers to questions b through f:

    a. Start the computer. Enter your user name and password if prompted to do so.

    b. Click the Start button. How many menu options are on the Start menu? *13*

    c. Run the program Calculator program located on the Programs, Accessories menu. How many buttons are now on the taskbar? *3*

    d. Run the Paint program and maximize the Paint window. How many application programs are running now? *2*

    e. Switch to Calculator. What are the two visual clues that tell you that Calculator is the active program? *The indented button close to star button. the calculator window.*

    f. Multiply 576 by 1457. What is the result? *839232*

    g. Close Calculator, then close Paint.

2. WordPad Help In Tutorial 1 you learned how to use Windows 95 Help. Just about every Windows 95 program has a help feature. Many computer users can learn to use a program just by using Help. To use Help, you would start the program, then click the Help menu at the top of the screen. Try using WordPad Help and complete steps a, b, and c:

    a. Start WordPad.

    b. Click Help on the WordPad menu bar, then click Help Topics.

    c. Using WordPad help, write out your answers to questions 1 through 3.

       1. How do you create a bulleted list? *Create*

       2. How do you set the margins in a document?

       3. What happens if you hold down the Alt key and press the Print Screen key?

3. Using Help to Explore Paint In this assignment, you will use the Paint Help to learn how to use the Paint program. Your goal is to create and print a picture that looks like the one in Figure 1-23.

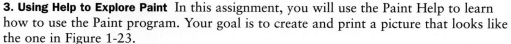

1) 1) create where you want the bulleted list to start. 2) on the format menu, click Bullet style, and then type your text. when you press enter another bullet appears on the next line. 3) to end the Bulleted list, click Bullet style again.

2) To set page margins on the file menu, click page setup, and then enter new values under margins.

3) Nothing ?

Figure 1-23 ◄

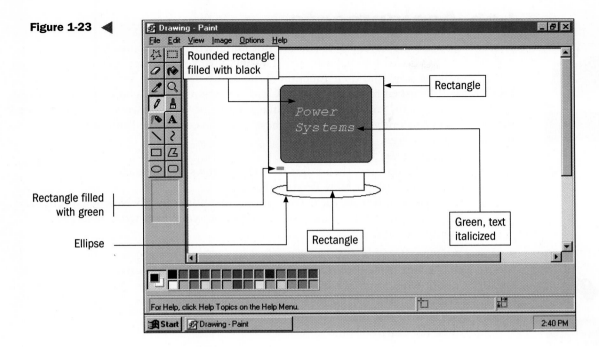

Rounded rectangle filled with black

Rectangle

Rectangle filled with green

Ellipse

Rectangle

Green, text italicized

a. Start Paint.

b. Click Help, then click Help Topics.

c. Use Paint Help to learn how to put text in a picture and how to draw rectangles and circles.

d. Draw a picture of a monitor using rectangles, circles, and text as shown in Figure 1-23.

e. Print your picture.

4. The Windows 95 Tutorial Windows 95 includes a five part on-line tutorial. In Tutorial 1 you learned about starting programs, switching windows, and using Help. You can use the on-line Windows 95 Tutorial to review what you learned and pick up some new tips for using Windows 95. Complete the following steps and write out your answers to questions f, g, and h:

a. Click the Start button to display the Start menu.

b. Click Help to display Windows help.

c. Click the Contents tab.

d. From the Contents screen, click Tour: Ten minutes to using Windows.

e. Click the Display button. If an error message appears, the Tour is probably not loaded on your computer. You will not be able to complete this assignment. Click Cancel, then click OK to cancel and check with your instructor or technical support person.

f. Click Starting a Program and complete the tutorial. What are the names of the seven programs on the Accessories menu in the tutorial?

g. Click Switching Windows and complete the on-line tutorial. What does the Minimize button do?

h. Click Using Help and complete the tutorial. What is the purpose of the [?] button?

i. Click the Exit button to close the Tour window.

j. Click the Exit Tour button to exit the Tour and return to the Windows 95 desktop.

Lab Assignments

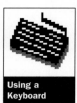

Using a Keyboard

1. Learning to Use the Keyboard If you are not familiar with computer keyboards, you will find the Keyboard Lab helpful. This Lab will give you a structured introduction to special computer keys and their function in Windows 95. As you work through the Lab, you will be asked to answer Quick Check questions about what you have learned. At the end of the lab, you will see a summary report of your answers. If your instructor wants you to print out your answers to these questions, click the Print button on the summary report screen.

   a. Click the Start button.

   b. Point to Programs, then point to CTI Windows 95 Applications.

   c. Click Windows 95 New Perspectives Brief.

   d. Click Using a Keyboard. If you cannot find Windows 95 New Perspectives Brief or Using a Keyboard, ask for help from your instructor or technical support person.

Using a Mouse

2. Mouse Practice If you would like more practice using a mouse, you can complete the Mouse Lab. As you work through the Lab, you will be asked to answer Quick Check questions about what you have learned. At the end of the lab, the Quick Check Report shows you how you did. If your instructor wants you to print out your answers to these questions, click the Print button on the summary report screen.

   a. Click the Start button.

   b. Point to Programs, then point to CTI Windows 95.

   c. Point to Windows 95 New Perspectives Brief.

   d. Click Using a Mouse. If you cannot find Windows 95 New Perspectives Brief or Using a Mouse, ask for help from your instructor or technical support person.

Working with Files

In this tutorial you will learn to:

■ Format a disk

■ Enter, select, insert, and delete text

■ Create and save a file

■ Open and edit a file

■ Print a file

■ Create a Student Disk

■ View the list of files on your disk

■ Move, copy, delete, and rename a file

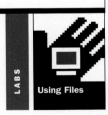

LABS

Using Files

CASE

Your First Day in the Lab—Continued

Steve Laslow is back from class, grinning. "I see you're making progress!"

"That's right," you reply. "I know how to run programs, control windows, and use Help. I guess I'm ready to work with my word-processing and spreadsheet software now."

Steve hesitates before he continues, "You could, but there are a few more things about Windows 95 that you should learn first."

Steve explains that most of the software you have on your computer—your word-processing, spreadsheet, scheduling, and graphing software—was created especially for the Windows 95 operating system. This software is referred to as **Windows 95 applications** or **Windows 95 programs**. You can also use software designed for Windows 3.1, but Windows 95 applications give you more flexibility. For example, when you name a document in a Windows 95 application, you can use descriptive filenames with up to 255 characters, whereas in Windows 3.1 you are limited to eight-character names.

You typically use Windows 95 applications to create files. A **file** is a collection of data that has a name and is stored in a computer. You typically create files that contain documents, pictures, and graphs when you use software packages. For example, you might use word-processing software to create a file containing a document. Once you create a file, you can open it, edit its contents, print it, and save it again—usually using the same application program you used to create it.

Another advantage of Windows 95 is that once you know how to save, open, and print files with one Windows 95 application, you can perform those same functions in *any* Windows 95 application. This is because Windows 95 applications have similar controls. For example, your word-processing and spreadsheet software will have identical menu commands to save, open, and print documents. Steve suggests that it would be worth a few minutes of your time to become familiar with these menus in Windows 95 applications.

You agree, but before you can get to work, Steve gives you one final suggestion: you should also learn how to keep track of the files on your disk. For instance, you might need to find a file you have not used for a while or you might want to delete a file if your disk is getting full. You will definitely want to make a backup copy of your disk in case something happens to the original. Steve's advice seems practical, and you're eager to explore these functions so you can get to work!

Tutorial 2 will help you learn how to work with Windows 95 applications and keep track of the files on your disk. When you've completed this tutorial, you'll be ready to tackle all kinds of Windows 95 software!

SESSION

2.1

In Session 2.1 you will learn how to format a disk so it can store files. You will create, save, open, and print a file. You will find out how the insertion point is different from the mouse pointer, and you will learn the basic skills for Windows 95 text entry, such as inserting, deleting, and selecting.
For this session you will need two blank 3 ½-inch disks.

Formatting a Disk

Before you can save files on a disk, the disk must be formatted. When the computer **formats** a disk, the magnetic particles on the disk surface are arranged so data can be stored on the disk. Today, many disks are sold preformatted and can be used right out of the box. However, if you purchase an unformatted disk, or if you have an old disk that you want to completely erase and reuse, you can format the disk using the Windows 95 Format command.

The following steps tell you how to format a 3 ½-inch high-density disk using drive A. Your instructor will tell you how to revise the instructions given in these steps if the procedure is different for your lab equipment.

All data on the disk you format will be erased, so don't perform these steps using a disk that contains important files.

To format a disk:

1. Start Windows 95, if necessary.

2. Write your name on the label of a 3 ½-inch disk.

3. Insert your disk in drive A. See Figure 2-1.

Figure 2-1 ◀
Inserting a
disk into the
disk drive

floppy disk drive

edge with the
notch goes into
the drive first

edge with the
label goes
in last

TROUBLE? If your disk does not fit in drive A, put it in drive B and substitute drive B for drive A in all of the steps for the rest of the tutorial.

4. Click the **My Computer** icon to select it, then press the **Enter** key. Make sure you can see the My Computer window. See Figure 2-2.

TROUBLE? If you see a list instead of icons like those in Figure 2-2, click View. Then click Large Icon.

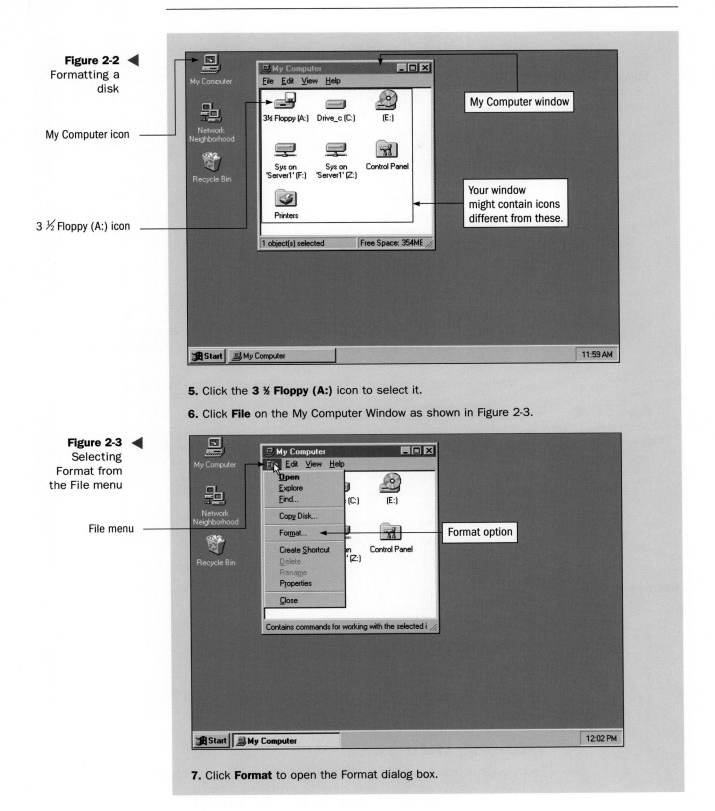

Figure 2-2 ◀
Formatting a
disk

My Computer icon

3 ½ Floppy (A:) icon

5. Click the **3 ½ Floppy (A:)** icon to select it.

6. Click **File** on the My Computer Window as shown in Figure 2-3.

Figure 2-3 ◀
Selecting
Format from
the File menu

File menu

7. Click **Format** to open the Format dialog box.

8. Make sure the dialog box settings on your screen match those in Figure 2-4.

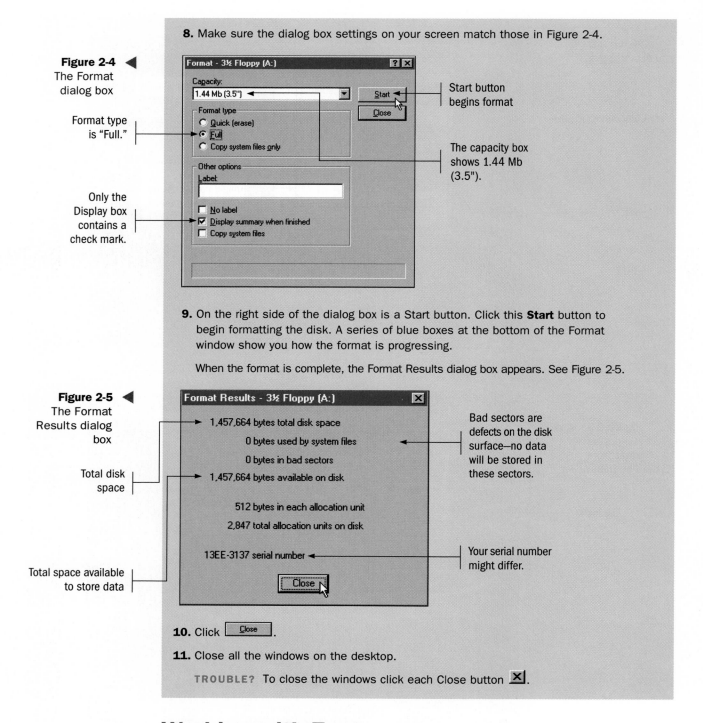

Figure 2-4 ◀
The Format dialog box

Format type is "Full."

Only the Display box contains a check mark.

Start button begins format

The capacity box shows 1.44 Mb (3.5").

9. On the right side of the dialog box is a Start button. Click this **Start** button to begin formatting the disk. A series of blue boxes at the bottom of the Format window show you how the format is progressing.

When the format is complete, the Format Results dialog box appears. See Figure 2-5.

Figure 2-5 ◀
The Format Results dialog box

Total disk space

Total space available to store data

Bad sectors are defects on the disk surface—no data will be stored in these sectors.

Your serial number might differ.

10. Click [Close].

11. Close all the windows on the desktop.

TROUBLE? To close the windows click each Close button ✖.

Working with Text

To accomplish many computing tasks, you need to type text in documents and text boxes. Windows 95 facilitates basic text entry by providing a text-entry area, by showing you where your text will appear on the screen, by helping you move around on the screen, and by providing insert and delete functions.

When you type sentences and paragraphs of text, do *not* press the Enter key when you reach the right margin. The software contains a feature called **word wrap** that automatically continues your text on the next line. Therefore, you should press Enter only when you have completed a paragraph.

If you type the wrong character, press the Backspace key to backup and delete the character. You can also use the Delete key. What's the difference between the Backspace and the Delete keys? The Backspace key deletes the character to left. The Delete key deletes the character to the right.

Now you will type some text using WordPad to learn about text entry.

To type text in WordPad:

1. Start WordPad.

    TROUBLE? If the WordPad window does not fill the screen, click the Maximize button 🔳.

2. Notice the flashing vertical bar, called the **insertion point**, in the upper-left corner of the document window. The insertion point indicates where the characters you type will appear.

3. Type your name, using the Shift key to type uppercase letters and using the spacebar to type spaces, just like on a typewriter.

4. Press the **Enter** key to end the current paragraph and move the insertion point down to the next line.

5. As you type the following sentences, watch what happens when the insertion point reaches the right edge of the screen:

    This is a sample typed in WordPad. See what happens when the insertion point reaches the right edge of the screen.

    TROUBLE? If you make a mistake, delete the incorrect character(s) by pressing the Backspace key on your keyboard. Then type the correct character(s).

The Insertion Point versus the Pointer

The insertion point is not the same as the mouse pointer. When the mouse pointer is in the text-entry area, it is called the **I-beam pointer** and looks like I. Figure 2-6 explains the difference between the insertion point and the I-beam pointer.

Figure 2-6 ◀
The insertion point vs. the pointer

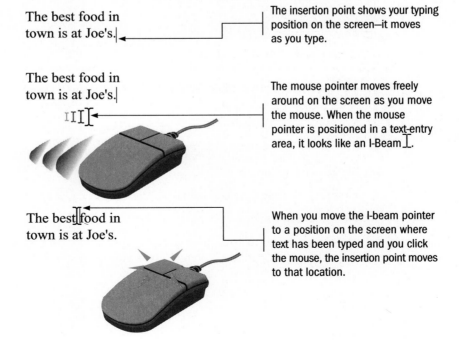

The best food in town is at Joe's.|

The insertion point shows your typing position on the screen—it moves as you type.

The best food in town is at Joe's.|

The mouse pointer moves freely around on the screen as you move the mouse. When the mouse pointer is positioned in a text-entry area, it looks like an I-Beam I.

The best food in town is at Joe's.

When you move the I-beam pointer to a position on the screen where text has been typed and you click the mouse, the insertion point moves to that location.

To move the insertion point:

1. Check the location of the insertion point and the I-beam pointer. The insertion point should be at the end of the sentence you typed in the last set of steps.

TROUBLE? If you don't see the I-beam pointer, move your mouse until you see it.

2. Use the mouse to move the I-beam pointer to the word "sample," then click the left mouse button. The insertion point jumps to the location of the I-beam pointer.

3. Move the I-beam pointer to a blank area near the bottom of the work space and click the left mouse button. *Notice that the insertion point does not jump to the location of the I-beam pointer.* Instead the insertion point jumps to the end of the last sentence. The insertion point can move only within existing text. It cannot be moved out of the existing text area.

Selecting Text

Many text operations are performed on a **block** of text, which is one or more consecutive words, sentences, or paragraphs. Once you select a block of text, you can delete it, move it, replace it, underline it, and so on. As you select a block of text, the computer highlights it. If you want to remove the highlighting, just click in the margin of your document.

Suppose you want to replace the phrase "See what happens" with "You can watch word wrap in action." You do not have to delete the text one character at a time. Instead you can highlight the entire phrase and begin to type the replacement text.

To select and replace a block of text:

1. Move the I-beam pointer just to the left of the word "See."

2. While holding down the left mouse button, drag the I-beam pointer over the text to the end of the word "happens." The phrase "See what happens" should now be highlighted. See Figure 2-7.

Figure 2-7 ◄
Highlighting
text

Position the
I-beam pointer here.

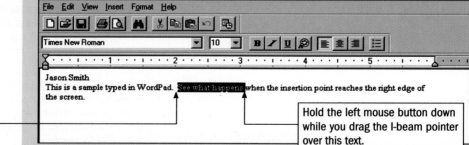

3. Release the left mouse button.

TROUBLE? If the phrase is not highlighted correctly, repeat Steps 1 through 3.

4. Type: **You can watch word wrap in action**

The text you typed replaces the highlighted text. Notice that you did not need to delete the highlighted text before you typed the replacement text.

Inserting a Character

Windows 95 programs usually operate in **insert mode**—when you type a new character, all characters to the right of the cursor are pushed over to make room.

Suppose you want to insert the word "sentence" before the word "typed."

To insert characters:

1. Position the I-beam pointer just before the word "typed," then click.

2. Type: **sentence**.

3. Press the **spacebar**.

3.I NOTE

When you save a file with a long filename, Windows 95 also creates an eight-character filename that can be used by Windows 3.1 applications. The eight-character filename is created by using the first six non-space characters from the long filename, then adding a tilde (~) and a number. For example, the filename Car Sales for 1997 would be converted to Carsal~1.

Notice how the letters in the first line are pushed to the right to make room for the new characters. When a word gets pushed past the right margin, the word-wrap feature pushes it down to the beginning of the next line.

Saving a File

As you type text, it is held temporarily in the computer's memory. For permanent storage, you need to save your work on a disk. In the computer lab, you will probably save your work on a floppy disk in drive A.

When you save a file, you must give it a name. Windows 95 allows you to use filenames containing up to 255 characters, and you may use spaces and punctuation symbols. You cannot use the symbols \ ? : * " < > | in a filename, but other symbols such as &, -, and $ are allowed.

Most filenames have an extension. An **extension** is a suffix of up to three characters that is separated from the filename by a period, as shown in Figure 2-8.

Figure 2-8 ◀
Filename and extension

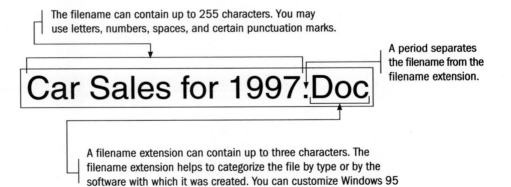

The filename can contain up to 255 characters. You may use letters, numbers, spaces, and certain punctuation marks.

A period separates the filename from the filename extension.

Car Sales for 1997.Doc

A filename extension can contain up to three characters. The filename extension helps to categorize the file by type or by the software with which it was created. You can customize Windows 95 to show the filename extension or to hide it.

The file extension indicates which application you used to create the file. For example, files created with Microsoft Word software have a .Doc extension. In general, you will not add an extension to your filenames, because the application software automatically does this for you.

Windows 95 keeps track of file extensions, but does not always display them. The steps in these tutorials refer to files using the filename, but not its extension. So if you see the filename Sample Text in the steps, but "Sample Text.Doc" on your screen, don't worry—these are the same files.

Now you can save the document you typed.

To save a document:

1. Click the **Save** button 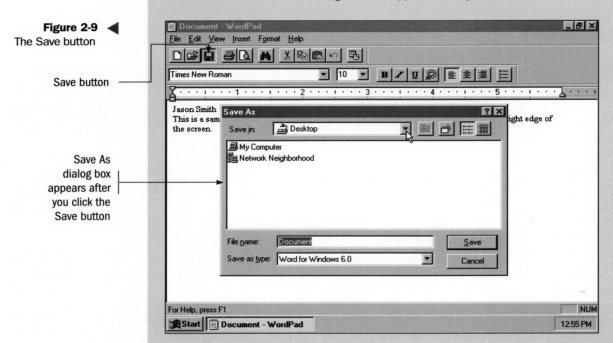 on the toolbar. Figure 2-9 shows the location of this button and the Save As dialog box that appears after you click it.

Figure 2-9 ◄
The Save button

Save button

Save As dialog box appears after you click the Save button

2. Click ▼ on the side of the Save in: box to display a list of drives. See Figure 2-10.

Figure 2-10 ◄
Selecting the drive

3 ½ Floppy (A:) drive menu option

Down Arrow button on the Save In box

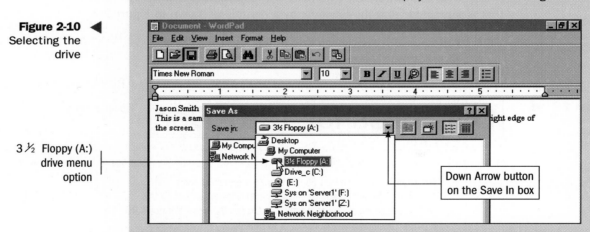

3. Click **3½ Floppy (A:).**

4. Select the text in the File Name box.

   TROUBLE? To select the text, position the I-beam pointer at the beginning of the word "Document." While you hold down the mouse button, drag the I-beam pointer to the end of the word.

5. Type **Sample Text** in the File Name box.

6. Click the **Save** button. Your file is saved on your Student Disk and the document title, "Sample Text," appears on the WordPad title bar.

What if you tried to close WordPad *before* you saved your file? Windows 95 would display a message—"Save changes to Document?" If you answer "Yes," Windows displays the Save As dialog box so you can give the document a name. If you answer "No," Windows 95 closes WordPad without saving the document.

After you save a file, you can work on another document or close WordPad. Since you have already saved your Sample Text document, you should continue this tutorial by closing WordPad.

To close WordPad:

1. Click the **Close** button ☒ to close the WordPad window.

Opening a File

Suppose you save and close the Sample Text file, then later you want to revise it. To revise a file you must first open it. When you **open** a file, its contents are copied into the computer's memory. If you revise the file, you need to save the changes before you close the application or work on a different file. If you close a revised file without saving your changes, you will lose the revisions.

Typically, you would use one of two methods to open a file. You could select the file from the Documents list or the My Computer window, or you could start an application program and then use the Open button to open the file. Each method has advantages and disadvantages. You will have an opportunity to try both methods.

The first method for opening the Sample Text file simply requires you to select the file from the Documents list or the My Computer window. With this method the document, not the application program, is central to the task; hence this method is sometimes referred to as *document-centric*. You only need to remember the name of your document or file—you do not need to remember which application you used to create the document.

The Documents list contains the names of the last 15 documents used. You access this list from the Start menu. When you have your own computer, the Documents list is very handy. In a computer lab, however, the files other students use quickly replace yours on the list.

If your file is not in the Documents list, you can open the file by selecting it from the My Computer window. Windows 95 starts an application program that you can use to revise the file, then automatically opens the file. The advantage of this method is its simplicity. The disadvantage is that Windows 95 might not start the application you expect. For example, when you select Sample Text, you might expect Windows 95 to start WordPad because you used WordPad to type the text of the document. Depending on the software installed on your computer system, however, Windows 95 might start the Microsoft Word application instead. Usually this is not a problem. Although the application might not be the one you expect, you can still use it to revise your file.

To open the Sample Text file by selecting it from My Computer:

1. Click the **My Computer** icon. Press the **Enter** key. The My Computer window opens.

2. Click the **3½ Floppy (A:)** icon, then press the **Enter** key. The 3½ Floppy (A:) window opens.

TROUBLE? If the My Computer window disappears when you open the 3½ floppy (A:) window, click View, click Options, then click the Folder tab, if necessary. Click the radio button labelled "Browse Folders using a separate window for each folder." Then click the OK button.

3. Click the **Sample Text** file icon, then press the **Enter** key. Windows 95 starts an application program, then automatically opens the Sample Text file.

TROUBLE? If Windows 95 starts Microsoft Word instead of WordPad, don't worry. You can use Microsoft Word to revise the Sample Text document.

3.1 NOTE

Document-centric features are advertised as an advantage of Windows 95. But you can still successfully use the application-centric approach you used with Windows 3.1 by opening your application, then opening your document.

Now that Windows 95 has started an application and opened the Sample Text file, you could make revisions to the document. Instead, you should close all the windows on your desktop so you can try the other method for opening files.

To close all the windows on the desktop:

1. Click ☒ on each of the windows.

   TROUBLE? If you see a message, "Save changes to Document?" click the No button.

The second method for opening the Sample Text file requires you to open WordPad, then use the Open button to select the Sample Text file. The advantage of this method is that you can specify the application program you want to use—WordPad in this case. This method, however, involves more steps than the method you tried previously.

To start WordPad and open the Sample Text file using the Open button:

1. Start WordPad.

2. Click the **Open** button ☐ on the toolbar. Figure 2-11 shows the location of this button and the dialog box that appears after you click it.

Figure 2-11 ◀
The Open button
and dialog box

Open button ─

Open dialog box ─

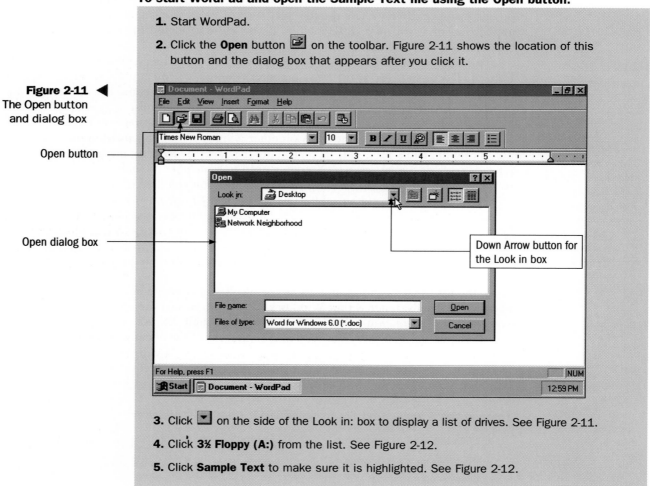

Down Arrow button for
the Look in box

3. Click ▼ on the side of the Look in: box to display a list of drives. See Figure 2-11.

4. Click **3½ Floppy (A:)** from the list. See Figure 2-12.

5. Click **Sample Text** to make sure it is highlighted. See Figure 2-12.

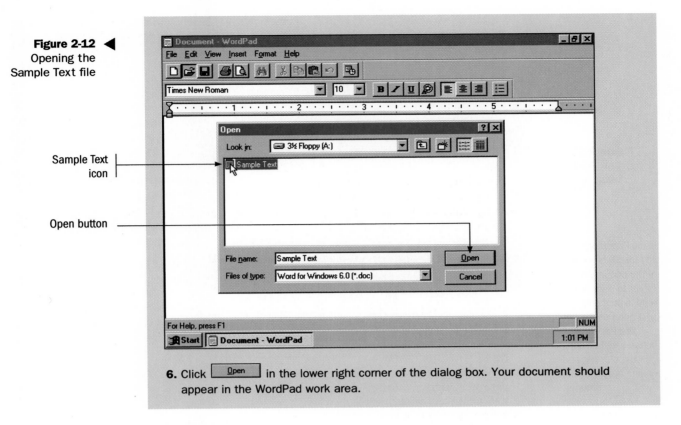

Figure 2-12 ◀
Opening the
Sample Text file

Sample Text
icon

Open button

6. Click [Open] in the lower right corner of the dialog box. Your document should appear in the WordPad work area.

Printing a File

Now that the Sample Text file is open, you can print it. It is a good idea to use Print Preview before you send your document to the printer. **Print Preview** shows on screen exactly how your document will appear on paper. You can check your page layout so you don't waste paper printing a document that is not quite the way you want it. Your instructor or technical support person might supply you with additional instructions for printing in your school's computer lab.

To preview, then print the Sample Text file:

1. Click the **Print Preview** button 🔍 on the toolbar.

2. Look at your print preview. Before you print the document and use paper, you should make sure that the font, margins, and other document features look the way you want them to.

   TROUBLE? If you can't read the document text on screen, click the Zoom In button.

3. Click the **Print** button. A Print dialog box appears.

4. Study Figure 2-13 to familiarize yourself with the controls in the Print dialog box.

This is the name of the printer that Windows 95 will use for this printout. If you are using a network, you might have a choice of printers. If you need to select a different printer, ask your instructor or your technical support person for help.

Figure 2-13 ◄
The Print
dialog box

The Properties button lets you modify the way your printer is set up. Do not change any of the settings on your school printer without the consent of your instructor or technical support person.

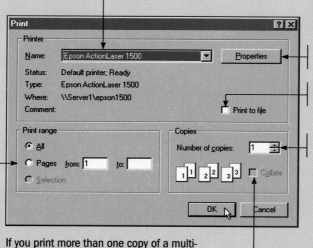

When you click this check box, your printout will go on your disk instead of to the printer.

In the Print range box, you specify how much of the document you want to print. If you want to print only part of a document, click the Pages radio button and then enter the starting and ending pages for the printout.

You can specify how many copies you want by typing the number in this box. Alternatively, you can use the arrow buttons to increase or decrease the number in the box.

If you print more than one copy of a multi-page document, you can specify that you want the printout collated, so you don't have to collate the pages manually.

5. Make sure your screen shows the Print range set to "All" and the number of copies set to "1."

6. Click the **OK** button to print your document. If a message appears telling you printing is complete, click the **OK** button.

TROUBLE? If your document does not print, make sure the printer has paper and the printer on-line light is on. If your document still doesn't print, ask your instructor or technical support person for help.

7. Close WordPad.

TROUBLE? If you see the message "Save changes to Document?" click the "No" button.

Quick Check

1. A(n) _____ is a collection of data that has a name and is stored on a disk or other storage medium.

2. _____ erases all the data on a disk and arranges the magnetic particles on the disk surface so the disk can store data.

3. When you are working in a text box, the pointer shape changes to a(n) _____.

4. The _____ shows you where each character you type will appear.

5. _____ automatically moves text down to the beginning of the next line when you reach the right margin.

6. Explain how you select a block of text: _____.

7. Which of these characters are not allowed in Windows 95 file names: \ ? : * " < > | ! @ # $ % ^ & ; + - ( ) /

⑧ In the filename New Equipment.Doc, .Doc is a(n) ——————.

⑨ Suppose you created a graph using the Harvard Graphics software and then you stored the graph on your floppy disk under the name Projected 1997 Sales - Graph. The next day, you use Harvard Graphics to open the file and change the graph. If you want the new version of the file on your disk, you need to ——————.

⑩ You can save —————— by using the Print Preview feature.

SESSION

2.2

In this session, you will learn how to manage the files on your disk—a skill that can prevent you from losing important documents. You will learn how to list information about the files on your disk; organize the files into folders; and move, delete, copy, and rename files.

Creating Your Student Disk

For this session of the tutorial, you must create a Student Disk that contains some sample files. *You can use the disk you formatted in the previous session.*

If you are using your own computer, the CTI Windows 95 Applications menu selection will not be available. Before you proceed, you must go to your school's computer lab and find a computer that has the CTI Windows 95 Applications installed. Once you have made your own Student Disk, you can use it to complete this tutorial on any computer you choose.

To add the sample files to your Student Disk:

1. Write "Windows 95 Student Disk" on the label of your formatted disk.

2. Place the disk in Drive A.

   TROUBLE? If your 3½-inch disk drive is B, place your formatted disk in that drive instead, and for the rest of this session substitute Drive B where ever you see Drive A.

3. Click the **Start** button [Start]. See Figure 2-14.

Figure 2-14 ◀
Making your
Student Disk

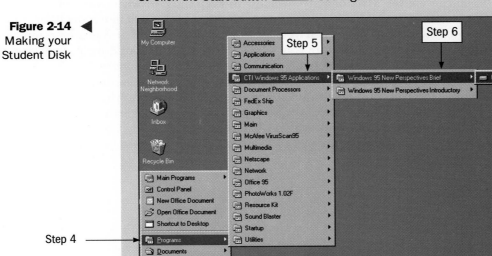

4. Point to **Programs.**

5. Point to **CTI Windows 95 Applications.**

TROUBLE? If CTI Windows 95 Applications is not listed, contact your instructor or technical support person.

6. Point to **Windows 95 New Perspectives Brief.**

7. Select **Make Student Disk.**

A dialog box opens, asking you to indicate the drive that contains your formatted disk.

8. If it is not already selected, click the Drive radio button that corresponds to the drive containing your student disk.

9. Click the **OK** button.

The sample files are copied to your formatted disk. A message tells you when all the files have been copied.

10. Click **OK.**

11. If necessary, close all the open windows on your screen.

Your Student Disk now contains sample files that you will use throughout the rest of this tutorial.

My Computer

The **My Computer** icon represents your computer, its storage devices, and its printers. The My Computer icon opens into the My Computer window, which contains an icon for each of the storage devices on your computer. On most computer systems the My Computer window also contains Control Panel and Printers folders, which help you add printers, control peripheral devices, and customize your Windows 95 work environment. Figure 2-15 on the following page explains more about the My Computer window.

You can use the My Computer window to keep track of where your files are stored and to organize your files. In this section of the tutorial you will move and delete files on your Student Disk in drive A. If you use your own computer at home or computer at work, you would probably store your files on drive C, instead of drive A. However, in a school lab environment you usually don't know which computer you will use, so you need to carry your files with you on a floppy disk that you use in drive A. In this session, therefore, you will learn how to work with the files on drive A. Most of what you learn will also work on your home or work computer when you use drive C.

In this session you will work with several icons, including My Computer. As a general procedure, when you want to open an icon, you click it and then press the Enter key.

Figure 2-15 ◀
Information
about My
Computer

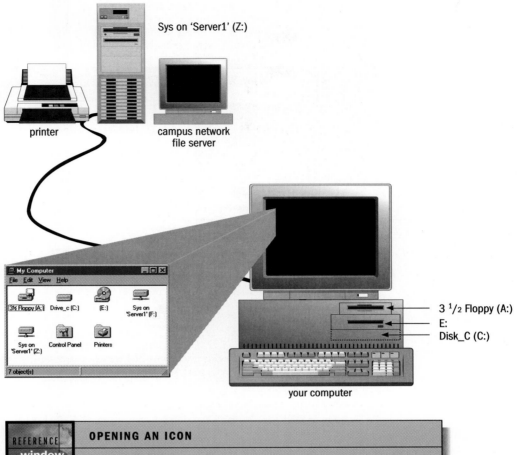

Sys on 'Server1' (Z:)

printer

campus network
file server

3 ½ Floppy (A:)
E:
Disk_C (C:)

your computer

REFERENCE **window**	**OPENING AN ICON**
	▪ Click the icon you want to open.
	▪ Press the Enter key.

Now you should open the My Computer icon.

To open the My Computer icon:

1. Click the **My Computer** icon to select it.

2. Press the **Enter** key. The My Computer window opens.

Now that you have opened the My Computer window, you can find out what is on
your Student Disk in drive A.

To find out what is on your Student Disk:

1. Open the **3½ Floppy (A:)** icon by clicking it, then pressing the **Enter** key. A window appears showing the contents of drive A:. See Figure 2-16.

Figure 2-16 ◄
Contents of
Student Disk

Icons show contents
of drive A

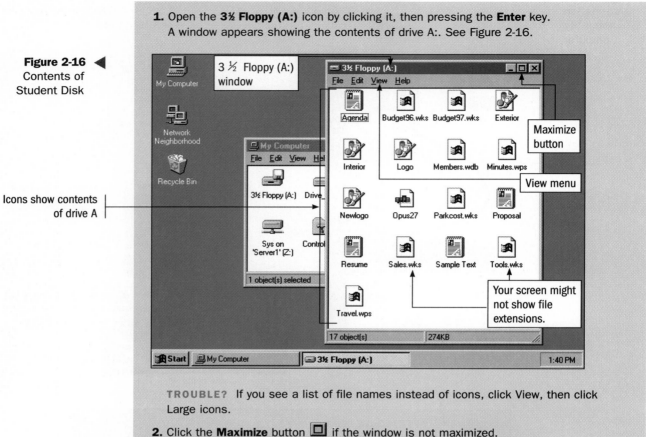

TROUBLE? If you see a list of file names instead of icons, click View, then click Large icons.

2. Click the **Maximize** button if the window is not maximized.

Windows 95 provides four ways to view the contents of a disk—large icons, small icons, list, or details. The standard view, shown on your screen, displays a large icon and title for each file. The icon provides a visual cue to the type and contents of the file, as Figure 2-17 illustrates.

Figure 2-17 ◄
Program and
file icons

Text files that you can open and read using the WordPad or NotePad software are represented by notepad icons.

The icons for Windows programs usually depict an object related to the function of the program. For example, an icon that looks like a calculator signifies the Windows Calc program; an icon that looks like a computer signifies the Windows Explorer program.

Many of the files you create are represented by page icons. Here the page icon for the Circles file shows some graphics tools to indicate the file contains a graphic. The Page icon for the Access file contains the Windows logo, indicating that Windows does not know if the file contains a document, graphics, or data base.

Folders provide a way to group and organize files. A folder icon contains other icons for folders and files. Here, the System folder contains files used by the Windows operating system.

Non-Windows programs are represented by this icon of a blank window.

The **Details** view shows more information than the large icon, small icon, and list views. Details view shows the file icon, the filename, the file size, the application you used to create the file, and the date/time the file was created or last modified.

To view a detailed list of files:

1. Click **View** then click **Details** to display details for the files on your disk as shown in Figure 2-18.

Figure 2-18 ◀
Detailed file list

File icon

Filename

Your screen might not
show file extensions

Total number of
files and folders
in the window

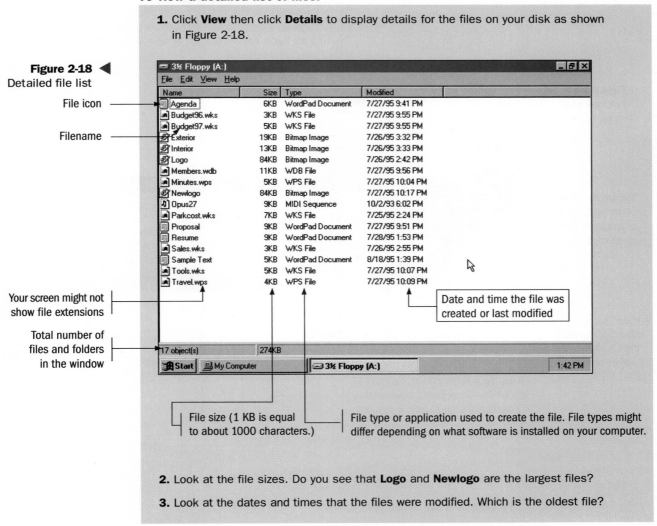

Date and time the file was
created or last modified

File size (1 KB is equal
to about 1000 characters.)

File type or application used to create the file. File types might
differ depending on what software is installed on your computer.

2. Look at the file sizes. Do you see that **Logo** and **Newlogo** are the largest files?

3. Look at the dates and times that the files were modified. Which is the oldest file?

Now that you have looked at the file details, switch back to the large icon view.

To switch to the large icon view:

1. Click **View** then click **Large Icons** to return to the large icon display.

Folders and Directories

A list of files is referred to as a **directory**. The main directory of a disk is sometimes called the **root directory**. The root directory is created when you format a disk and is shown in parentheses at the top of the window. For example, at the top of your screen you should see "3 ½ Floppy (A:)." The root directory is A:. In some situations, the root directory is indicated by a backslash after the drive letter and colon, such as A:\. All of the files on your Student Disk are currently in the root directory.

If too many files are stored in a directory, the directory list becomes very long and difficult to manage. A directory can be divided into **folders** (also called **subdirectories**), into which you group similar files. The directory of files for each folder then becomes much shorter and easier to manage. For example, you might create a folder for all the papers you write for an English 111 class as shown in Figure 2-19.

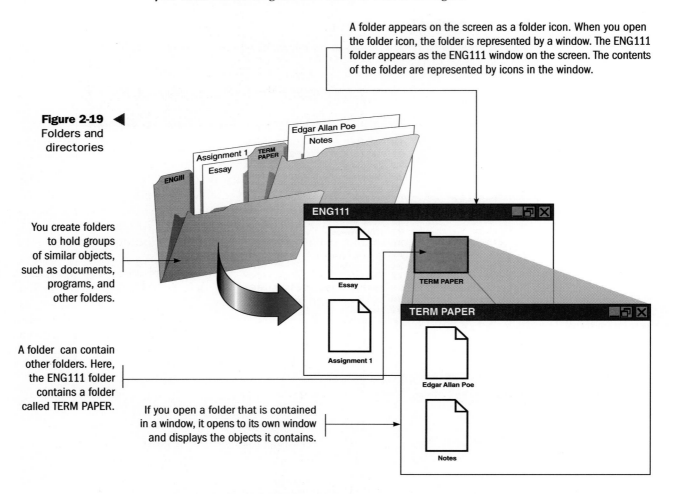

A folder appears on the screen as a folder icon. When you open the folder icon, the folder is represented by a window. The ENG111 folder appears as the ENG111 window on the screen. The contents of the folder are represented by icons in the window.

Figure 2-19 ◀
Folders and directories

You create folders to hold groups of similar objects, such as documents, programs, and other folders.

A folder can contain other folders. Here, the ENG111 folder contains a folder called TERM PAPER.

If you open a folder that is contained in a window, it opens to its own window and displays the objects it contains.

Now, you'll create a folder called My Documents to hold your document files.

To create a My Documents folder:

1. Click **File** then point to **New** to display the submenu.

2. Click **Folder**. A folder icon with the label "New Folder" appears.

3. Type **My Documents** as the name of the folder.

4. Press the **Enter** key.

When you first create a folder, it doesn't contain any files. In the next set of steps you will move a file from the root directory to the My Documents folder.

CREATING A NEW FOLDER

- Open the My Computer icon to display the My Computer window.
- Open the icon for the drive on which you want to create the folder.
- Click File then point to New.
- From the submenu click Folder.
- Type the name for the new folder.
- Press the Enter key.

Moving and Copying a File

You can move a file from one directory to another or from one disk to another. When you move a file it is copied to the new location you specify, then the version in the old location is erased. The move feature is handy for organizing or reorganizing the files on your disk by moving them into appropriate folders. The easiest way to move a file is to hold down the *right* mouse button and drag the file from the old location to the new location. A menu appears and you select Move Here.

You can also copy a file from one directory to another, or from one disk to another. When you copy a file, you create an exact duplicate of an existing file in whatever disk or folder you specify. To copy a file from one folder to another on your floppy disk, you use the same procedure as for moving a file, except that you select Copy Here from the menu.

Suppose you want to move the Minutes file from the root directory to the My Documents folder. Depending on the software applications installed on your computer, this file is either called Minutes or Minutes.wps. In the steps it is referred to simply as Minutes.

To move the Minutes file to the My Documents folder:

1. Click the **Minutes** icon to select it.

2. Press and hold the right mouse button while you drag the **Minutes** icon to the My Documents folder. See Figure 2-20.

Figure 2-20 ◄
Moving a file

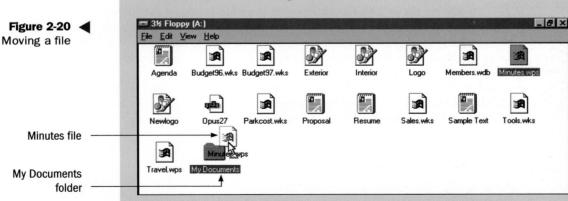

Minutes file

My Documents folder

3. Release the right mouse button. A menu appears.

4. Click **Move Here**. A short animation shows the Minutes file being moved to My Documents. The Minutes icon disappears from the window showing the files in the root directory.

MOVING A FILE

- Open the My Computer icon to display the My Computer window.
- If the document you want to move is in a folder, open the folder.
- Hold down the *right* mouse button while you drag the file icon to its new folder or disk location.
- Click Move Here.
- If you want to move more than one file at a time, hold down the Ctrl key while you click the icons for all the files you want to move.

3.1 NOTE

Windows 3.1 users be careful! When you delete or move an icon in the Windows 95 My Computer window you are actually deleting or moving the file. This is quite different from the way the Windows 3.1 Program Manager worked.

Anything you do to an icon in the My Computer window is actually done to the file represented by that icon. If you move an icon, the file is moved; if you delete an icon, the file is deleted.

After you move a file, it is a good idea to make sure it was moved to the correct location. You can easily verify that a file is in its new folder by displaying the folder contents.

To verify that the Minutes file was moved to My Documents:

1. Click the **My Documents** folder, then press **Enter**. The My Documents window appears and it contains one file—Minutes.

2. Click the My Documents window **Close** button ⊠.

   TROUBLE? If the My Computer window is no longer visible, click the My Computer icon, then press Enter. You might also need to open the 3 ½ Floppy (A:) icon.

Deleting a File

You delete a file or folder by deleting its icon. However, be careful when you delete a *folder*, because you also delete all the files it contains! When you delete a file from the hard drive, the filename is deleted from the directory but the file contents are held in the Recycle Bin. If you change your mind and want to retrieve the deleted file, you can recover it by clicking the Recycle Bin.

When you delete a file from a floppy disk, it does not go into the Recycle Bin. Instead it is deleted as soon as its icon disappears. Try deleting the file named Agenda from your Student Disk. Because this file is on the floppy disk and not on the hard disk, it will not go into the Recycle Bin.

To delete the file Agenda:

1. Click the icon for the file **Agenda**.

2. Press the **Delete** key.

3. If a message appears asking, "Are sure you want to delete Agenda?", click **Yes**. An animation, which might play too quickly to be seen, shows the file being deleted.

DELETING A FILE

■ Click the icon for the file you want to delete.
■ Press the Delete key.

Renaming a File

You can easily change the name of a file using the Rename option on the File menu or by using the file's label. Remember that when you choose a filename it can contain up to 255 characters, including spaces, but it cannot contain \ ? : " < > | characters.

Practice using this feature by renaming the Sales file to give it a more descriptive filename.

To rename Sales:

1. Click the **Sales** file to select it.

2. Click the label "Sales". After a short pause a solid box outlines the label and an insertion point appears.

3. Type **Preliminary Sales Summary** as the new filename.

4. Press the **Enter key**.

5. Click the **Close** button ☒ to close the 3 ½-inch Floppy (A:) window.

RENAMING A FILE

■ Click the icon for the file you want to rename.
■ Click the label of the icon.
■ Type the new name for the file.
■ Press the Enter key.

Copying an Entire Floppy Disk

You can have trouble accessing the data on your floppy disk if the disk gets damaged, exposed to magnetic fields, or picks up a computer virus. If the damaged disk contains important files, you will have to spend many hours to try to reconstruct those files. To avoid losing all your data, it is a good idea to make a copy of your floppy disk. This copy is called a **backup** copy.

If you wanted to make a copy of an audio cassette, your cassette player would need two cassette drives. You might wonder, therefore, how your computer can make a copy of your disk if you have only one disk drive. Figure 2-21 illustrates how the computer uses only one disk drive to make a copy of a disk.

Figure 2-21 ◀
Using one disk
drive to make a
copy of a disk

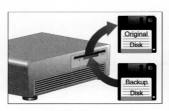

1. First, the computer
copies the data from your
original disk into memory.

2. Once the data is in
memory, you remove your
original disk from the drive
and replace it with your
backup disk.

3. The computer moves the
data from memory onto
your backup disk.

REFERENCE
window

MAKING A BACKUP OF YOUR FLOPPY DISK

- Click My Computer then press the Enter key.
- Insert the disk you want to copy in drive A.
- Click the 3 ½ Floppy (A:) icon   3½ Floppy (A:)   to select it.
- Click File then click Copy Disk to display the Copy Disk dialog box.
- Click Start to begin the copy process.
- When prompted, remove the disk you want to copy. Place your backup disk in drive A.
- Click OK.
- When the copy is complete, close the Copy Disk dialog box.
- Close the My Computer dialog box.

If you have two floppy disks, you can make a backup of your Student Disk now. Make sure you periodically follow the backup procedure, so your backup is up-to-date.

To back up your Student Disk:

1. Write your name and "Backup" on the label of your second disk. This will be your backup disk.

2. Make sure your Student Disk is in drive A.

3. Make sure the My Computer window is open. See Figure 2-22.

Figure 2-22 ◀
The My
Computer
window

4. Click the **3 ½ Floppy (A:)** icon 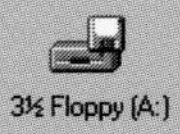 ⊡ to select it.

   TROUBLE? If you mistakenly open the 3½ Floppy (A:) *window,* click ⊠.

5. Click **File**.

6. Click **Copy Disk** to display the Copy Disk dialog box as shown in Figure 2-23.

Figure 2-23 ◀
The Copy Disk
dialog box

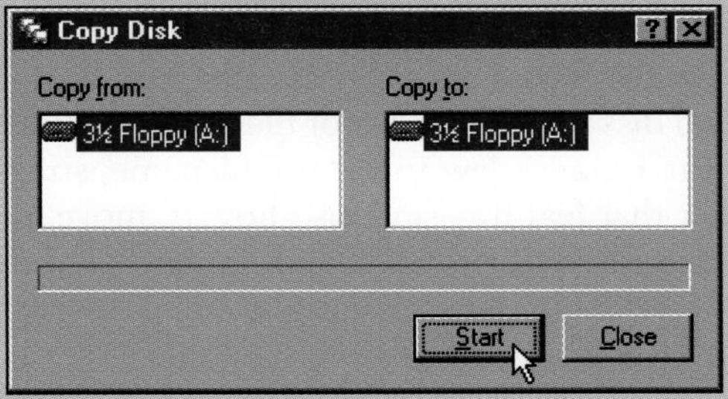

7. On the lower right side of the dialog box, you'll see a Start button. Click this
   Start button to begin the copy process.

8. When the message, "Insert the disk you want to copy from (source disk)..."
   appears, click the **OK** button.

9. When the message, "Insert the disk you want to copy to (destination disk)..."
   appears, insert your backup disk in drive A.

10. Click the **OK** button. When the copy is complete, you will see the message "Copy
    completed successfully."

11. After the data is copied to your backup disk, click ⊠ on the blue title bar of the
    Copy Disk dialog box.

12. Click ⊠ on the My Computer window to close the My Computer window.

13. Remove your disk from the drive.

   Each time you make a backup, the data on your backup disk is erased, and replaced
with the data from your updated Student Disk. Now that you know how to copy an entire
disk, make a backup whenever you have completed a tutorial or you have spent a long
time working on a file.

Quick Check

1. If you want to find out about the storage devices and printers connected to your computer, click the _____ icon.

2. If you have only one floppy disk drive on your computer, it is identified by the letter _____.

3. The letter C: is typically used for the _____ drive of a computer.

4. What are the five pieces of information that the Details view supplies about each of your files?

5. The main directory of a disk is referred to as the _____ directory.

6. You can divide a directory into _____.

7. If you delete the icon for a file, what happens to the file?

8. If you have one floppy disk drive, but you have two disks, can you copy a file from one floppy disk to another?

End Note

Just as you complete the Quick Check for Session 2.2, Steve appears. He asks how you are doing. You summarize what you remember from the tutorial, telling him that you learned how to insert, delete, and select text. You also learned how to work with files using Windows 95 software—you now know how to save, open, revise, and print a document. You tell him that you like the idea that these file operations are the same for almost all Windows 95 software. Steve agrees that this makes work a lot easier.

When Steve asks you if you have a supply of disks, you tell him you do, and that you just learned how to format a disk and view a list of files on your disk. Steve wants you to remember that you can use the Details view to see the filename, size, date, and time. You assure him that you remember that feature—and also how to move, delete, and rename a file.

Steve seems pleased with your progress and agrees that you're now ready to use software applications. But he can't resist giving you one last warning—don't forget to back up your files frequently!

Tutorial Assignments

1. Opening, Editing, and Printing a Document In this tutorial you learned how to create a document using WordPad. You also learned how to save, open, and print a document. Practice these skills by opening the document on your Student Disk called Resume, which is a résumé for Jamie Woods. Make the changes shown in Figure 2-24, and then print the document. After you print, save your revisions.

Figure 2-24 ◀

Change this to your
name, address, and
phone number. If you
don't have an office
number delete this.

Change this to the
name of your
university or college.

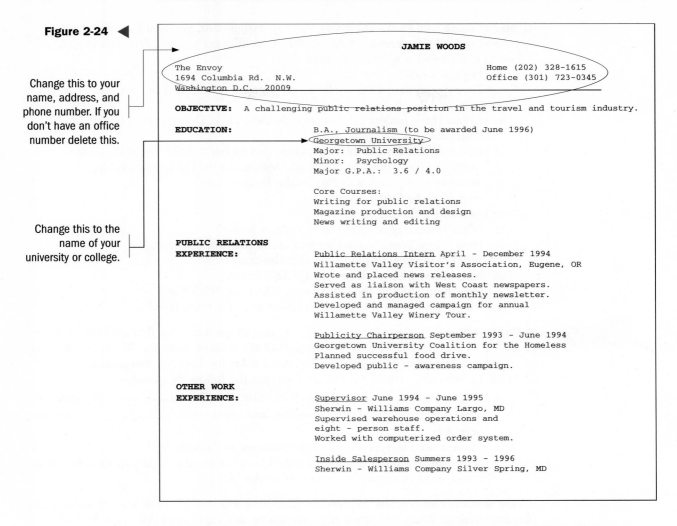

```
                                    JAMIE WOODS

The Envoy                                     Home (202) 328-1615
1694 Columbia Rd.  N.W.                       Office (301) 723-0345
Washington D.C.  20009

OBJECTIVE:    A challenging public relations position in the travel and tourism industry.

EDUCATION:              B.A., Journalism (to be awarded June 1996)
                        Georgetown University
                        Major:  Public Relations
                        Minor:  Psychology
                        Major G.P.A.:  3.6 / 4.0

                        Core Courses:
                        Writing for public relations
                        Magazine production and design
                        News writing and editing

PUBLIC RELATIONS
EXPERIENCE:             Public Relations Intern April - December 1994
                        Willamette Valley Visitor's Association, Eugene, OR
                        Wrote and placed news releases.
                        Served as liaison with West Coast newspapers.
                        Assisted in production of monthly newsletter.
                        Developed and managed campaign for annual
                        Willamette Valley Winery Tour.

                        Publicity Chairperson September 1993 - June 1994
                        Georgetown University Coalition for the Homeless
                        Planned successful food drive.
                        Developed public - awareness campaign.

OTHER WORK
EXPERIENCE:             Supervisor June 1994 - June 1995
                        Sherwin - Williams Company Largo, MD
                        Supervised warehouse operations and
                        eight - person staff.
                        Worked with computerized order system.

                        Inside Salesperson Summers 1993 - 1996
                        Sherwin - Williams Company Silver Spring, MD
```

2. Creating, Saving, and Printing a Letter Use WordPad to write a one-page letter to a relative or a friend. Save the document in the My Documents folder with the name "Letter." Use the Print Preview feature to look at the format of your finished letter, then print it, and be sure you sign it.

3. Managing Files and Folders Earlier in this tutorial you created a folder and moved the file called Minutes into it. Now complete a through g below to practice your file management skills.

    a. Create a folder called Spreadsheets on your Student Disk.

    b. Move the files ParkCost, Budget96, Budget97, and Sales into the Spreadsheets folder.

    c. Create a folder called Park Project.

    d. Move the files Proposal, Members, Tools, Logo, and Newlogo into the Park Project folder.

    e. Move the ParkCost file from the Spreadsheets folder to the Park Project folder.

    f. Delete the file called Travel.

    g. Switch to the Details view and answer the following questions:

Write out your answers to questions a through e.

    a. What is the largest file in the Park Project folder?

    b. What is the newest file in the Spreadsheets folder?

    c. How many files are in the root directory?

    d. How are the Members and Resume icons different?

    e. What is the file with the most recent date on the entire disk?

4. More Practice with Files and Folders For this assignment, you will format your disk again and put a fresh version of the Student Disk files on it. Complete a through h below to practice your file management skills.

    a. Format a disk.

    b. Create a Student Disk. Refer to the section "Creating Your Student Disk" in Session 2.2.

    c. Create three folders on your new Student Disk: Documents, Budgets, and Graphics.

    d. Move the files Interior, Exterior, Logo, and Newlogo to the Graphics folder.

    e. Move the files Travel, Members and Minutes to the Documents folder.

    f. Move Budget96 and Budget97 to the Budgets folder.

    g. Switch to the Details view.

Answer questions a through f.

    a. What is the largest file in the Graphics folder?

    b. How many WordPad documents are in the root directory?

    c. What is the newest file in the root directory?

    d. How many files in all folders are 5KB in size?

    e. How many files in the Documents folder are WKS files?

    f. Do all the files in the Graphics folder have the same icon?

5. Finding a File Microsoft Windows 95 contains an on-line Tour that explains how to find files on a disk without looking through all the folders. Start the Windows 95 Tour (if you don't remember how, look at the instructions for Tutorial Assignment 1 in Tutorial 1), then click Finding a File, and answer the following questions:

    a. To display the Find dialog box, you must click the _____ button, then select _____ from the menu, and finally click _____ from the submenu.

    b. Do you need to type in the entire filename to find the file?

    c. When the computer has found your file, what are the steps you have to follow if you want to display the contents of the file?

6. Help with Files and Folders In Tutorial 2 you learned how to work with Windows 95 files and folders. What additional information on this topic does Windows 95 Help provide? Use the Start button to access Help. Use the Index tab to locate topics related to files and folders. Find at least two tips or procedures for working with files and folders that were not covered in the tutorial. Write out the tip in your own words and indicate the title of the Help screen that contains the information.

Lab Assignments

1. Using Files Lab In Tutorial 2 you learned how to create, save, open, and print files. The Using Files Lab will help you review what happens in the computer when you perform these file tasks. To start the Lab, follow these steps:

    a. Click the Start button.

    b. Point to Programs, then point to CTI Windows 95 Applications.

    c. Point to Windows 95 New Perspectives Brief.

    d. Click Using Files. If you can't find Windows 95 New Perspectives Brief or Using Files, ask for help from your instructor or technical support person.

Answer the Quick Check questions that appear as you work through the Lab. You can print your answers at the end of the Lab.

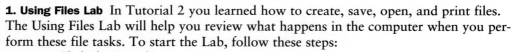
Using Files

Answers to Quick Check Questions

SESSION 1.1

1. a. icon b. Start button c. taskbar d. Date/Time control e. desktop f. pointer

2. Multitasking

3. Start menu

4. Lift up the mouse, move it to the right, then put it down, and slide it left until the pointer reaches the left edge of the screen.

5. Highlighting

6. If a program is running, its button is displayed on the taskbar.

7. Each program that is running uses system resources, so Windows 95 runs more efficiently when only the programs you are using are open.

8. Answer: If you do not perform the shut down procedure, you might lose data.

SESSION 1.2

1. a. title bar b. program title c. Minimize button d. Restore button e. Close button f. menu bar g. toolbar h. formatting bar i. taskbar j. status bar k. workspace l. pointer

2. a. Minimize button—hides the program so only its button is showing on the taskbar.
   b. Maximize button—enlarges the program to fill the entire screen.
   c. Restore button—sets the program to a pre-defined size.
   d. Close button—stops the program and removes its button from the taskbar.

3. a. Ellipses—indicate a dialog box will appear.
   b. Grayed out—the menu option is not currently available.
   c. Submenu—indicates a submenu will appear.
   d. Check mark—indicates a menu option is currently in effect.

4. Toolbar

5. a. scroll bar b. scroll box c. Cancel button d. down arrow button e. list box f. radio button g. check box

6. one, check boxes

7. On-line Help

SESSION 2.1

1. file

2. formatting

3. I-beam

4. insertion point

5. word wrap

6 | You drag the I-beam pointer over the text to highlight it.

7 | \ ? : * < > | "

8 | extension

9 | save the file again

10 | paper

SESSION 2.2

1 | My Computer

2 | A (or A:)

3 | Hard (or hard disk)

4 | Filename, file type, file size, date, time

5 | Root

6 | Folders (or subdirectories)

7 | It is deleted from the disk.

8 | Yes

Organizing Files with Windows Explorer

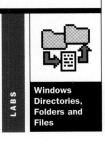

LABS

Windows Directories, Folders and Files

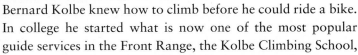

CASE

Kolbe Climbing School

Bernard Kolbe knew how to climb before he could ride a bike. In college he started what is now one of the most popular guide services in the Front Range, the Kolbe Climbing School, known to locals as "KCS." KCS offers guided climbs in the Front Range area, especially in Rocky Mountain National Park and nearby climbing areas such as Lumpy Ridge. While most clients simply want to learn rock and sport climbing, there are a few who want guides for longer alpine climbs and ice climbing.

Since he started his business, Bernard has handled the paperwork using yellow pads, clipboards, and manila folders. Recent conversations with his insurance agent and accountant, though, convinced him that he needs to keep better records on his employees, clients, and the use and condition of his equipment. The KCS offices adjoin a business services office, so Bernard for the first time rented some computer time and began creating the files he needs, storing them on a floppy disk.

Not too long ago, Bernard asked if you could help him out with KCS record-keeping. You agreed (in exchange for some free climbing lessons) and got to work by updating the client files on his floppy disk. When Bernard first gave you the disk he warned you that it could use a little organization, so you began by creating a folder structure on the disk.

This morning, though, you walked into the office to find that Bernard had spent yesterday evening at the rented computer adding new files to his disk. When you discover that he didn't bother to organize his work, you point out that an important part of computerized record-keeping is creating and using a system that makes it easy to find important information. Bernard is willing to learn more (it's too cold to climb anyway), so the two of you head over to the business services office to spend some time looking over Bernard's files.

SESSION

3.1

In this session, you will learn how Windows Explorer displays the devices and folders that your computer can access. Understanding how to manipulate this display of devices and folders is the first Step toward using Windows Explorer to organize the files on your disks. In this tutorial you will work with the files and folders on a floppy disk. When you have your own computer or are in a business environment, you will more likely work with files and folders on a hard disk drive. You will discover that file management techniques are the same for floppy disks and hard disks.

Preparing Your Student Disk with Quick Format

Before you begin, you need to create a new Student Disk that contains the sample files you will work with in Tutorials 3 and 4. You can make your Student Disk using the CTI Windows 95 Applications menu.

If you are using your own computer, the CTI Windows 95 Applications menu will *not* be available. Before you proceed, you must go to your school's computer lab and use the CTI Windows 95 Applications menu to make your new Student Disk. Once you have made the disk, you can use it to complete this tutorial on any computer that runs Windows 95.

If you still have the Student Disk from Tutorials 1 and 2 and don't need it any longer, you can reuse it for Tutorials 3 and 4. Otherwise, bring a blank, formatted disk to the lab.

When you want to erase the contents of a floppy disk, you can use the Quick format option rather than the Full format that you use on a new disk. A Quick format takes less time than a Full format because instead of preparing the entire disk surface, a Quick format erases something called the file allocation table. The **file allocation table (FAT)** stores the locations of all the files on the disk. By erasing the FAT, you erase all the information that tells the computer about the files on the disk and so the disk appears empty to the computer.

To Quick format your Student Disk:

1. Place your Student Disk in drive A.

> **TROUBLE?** If your 3½-inch disk drive is B, place your formatted disk in that drive instead, and for the rest of this tutorial substitute drive B wherever you see drive A.

2. Click the **My Computer** icon, then press **Enter** to open the My Computer window.

3. Click the **3½ Floppy (A:)** icon.

4. Click **File**, then click **Format** to display the Format dialog box.

5. Make sure the **Quick (erase)** button and other settings in the dialog box match those shown in Figure 3-1.

Figure 3-1
Format
dialog box

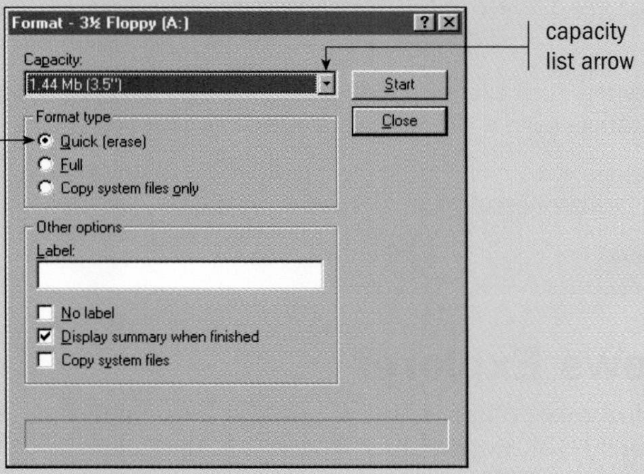

click to Quick
format a disk

capacity
list arrow

6. Click the **Start** button to begin the Quick format.

   TROUBLE? If an error message appears, it is possible your disk capacity is double-density instead of high-density. Click the Capacity list arrow, click 720 KB (3.5"), then repeat Step 6.

7. When the Format Results dialog box appears, click the **Close** button.

8. Click the **Close** button to close the Format dialog box.

Now that you have formatted your disk, you can make a Student Disk for Tutorials 3 and 4.

To create your Student Disk:

1. Click the **Start** button [Start], point to **Programs**, point to **CTI Windows 95 Applications**, point to **Windows 95 New Perspectives Introductory**, then click **Make Student Disk**. Figure 3-2 shows the Start menu structure you need to navigate.

Figure 3-2
Making your
Student Disk

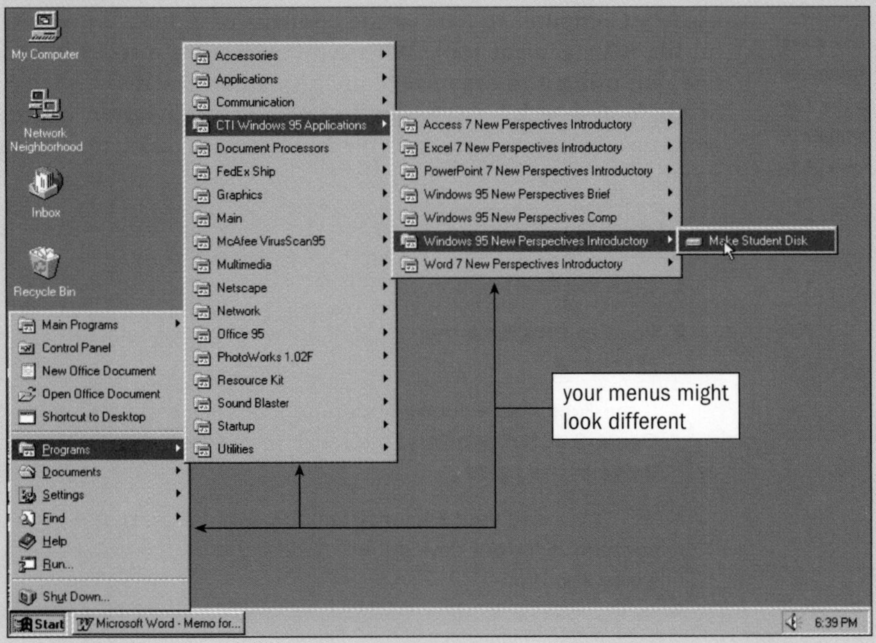

your menus might
look different

A dialog box opens, asking you to indicate the drive that contains your formatted disk.

2. Follow the instructions on the screen. The files are copied to your formatted disk. A message tells you when all the files have been copied.

3. Click the **OK** button. Your Student Disk now contains files that you will use throughout the rest of this tutorial.

4. Close all the open windows on your screen.

Windows Explorer

The root directory of Bernard's disk contains three folders plus the files he hasn't yet organized. Figure 3-3 shows the three folders and their contents.

Figure 3-3 ◀
Folders on
Bernard's disk

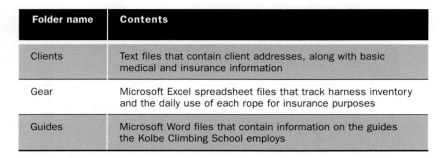

Folder name	Contents
Clients	Text files that contain client addresses, along with basic medical and insurance information
Gear	Microsoft Excel spreadsheet files that track harness inventory and the daily use of each rope for insurance purposes
Guides	Microsoft Word files that contain information on the guides the Kolbe Climbing School employs

Windows Directories, Folders and Files

3.1 NOTE

In many ways Windows Explorer is similar to the File Manager in Windows 3.1.

The files Bernard needs to organize are also in the root directory. The ideal tool for file organization tasks, you tell Bernard, is Windows Explorer.

Windows Explorer is a program included with Windows 95 that is designed to simplify disk management tasks such as locating, viewing, moving, copying, and deleting files or folders. Using a single window divided into two sections, Windows Explorer provides an easy-to-navigate representation of disks, folders, and files.

Windows 95 provides more than one way to accomplish most tasks. Although you can use My Computer to look at the contents of a disk, Windows Explorer is a more powerful file management tool. When you're moving just a file or two, My Computer works fine, but using it to organize many files on several disks often results in a frustrating game of "hide and seek" as you try to navigate on a screen cluttered with files, folders, and windows. For more advanced file management tasks, many people prefer to use Windows Explorer.

To start Windows Explorer:

1. Click the **Start** button 🏁 Start .

2. Point to **Programs** then click **Windows Explorer** to open a window titled "Exploring."

3. If the Exploring window is not maximized, click the **Maximize** button ▢ . See Figure 3-4, but don't try to arrange the folders and files on your screen to match those in the figure.

   TROUBLE? If your Exploring window lists look different, your computer probably contains different devices and folders than the ones shown in Figure 3-4. Don't worry about it.

Study Figure 3-4 and notice how the Exploring window is divided into two sections: a Folders list and a Contents list.

Figure 3-4
Windows
Explorer
overview

icon that represents
your floppy drive

folder icon

use this scroll bar
to scroll through
the Folders list

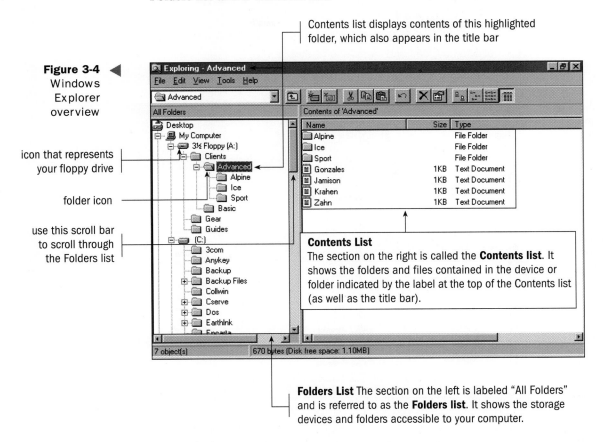

Contents list displays contents of this highlighted
folder, which also appears in the title bar

Contents List
The section on the right is called the **Contents list**. It shows the folders and files contained in the device or folder indicated by the label at the top of the Contents list (as well as the title bar).

Folders List The section on the left is labeled "All Folders" and is referred to as the **Folders list**. It shows the storage devices and folders accessible to your computer.

Notice the folders called Advanced and Basic in Figure 3-4. These two folders are contained in the folder called Clients. Folders that are contained in other folders are referred to as **subfolders**. The Advanced folder itself has subfolders: Alpine, Ice, and Sport. You might have noticed that both the Folders list and the Contents list display the Alpine, Ice, and Sport folders. To some people it is confusing that these folders are shown in both the Folders list and the Contents list. However, they are not duplicate folders; they are just shown twice. The Folders list displays a device's *structure*, that is, its levels of folders and subfolders. The Contents list, on the other hand, displays the *contents* of a device or folder, including its folders and its files.

To see the devices—drives, printers, and other objects—connected to your computer, you scroll through the Folders list. Each object in the list has a small icon next to it. Explorer uses the icons shown in Figure 3-5 to represent different types of storage devices.

Figure 3-5
Storage device
icons

Icon	Represents
	floppy disk drive
	hard disk drive on your computer
	CD-ROM drive
	network disk drive
	shared disk drive

To see a list of storage devices connected to your computer:

1. Drag the Folders list scroll box until you can see the 🖳 Desktop icon at the top. Refer to Figure 3-6 for the location of this scroll box.

   TROUBLE? If you don't have a scroll box, you don't have more than one screen of open devices and files. Skip to Step 3.

2. Scroll to the bottom of the Folders list. See Figure 3-6.

Figure 3-6 ◄
Devices and
folders in the
Folders list

Folders list shows the
devices and folders
accessible to your
computer system

drag to scroll through
the Folders list

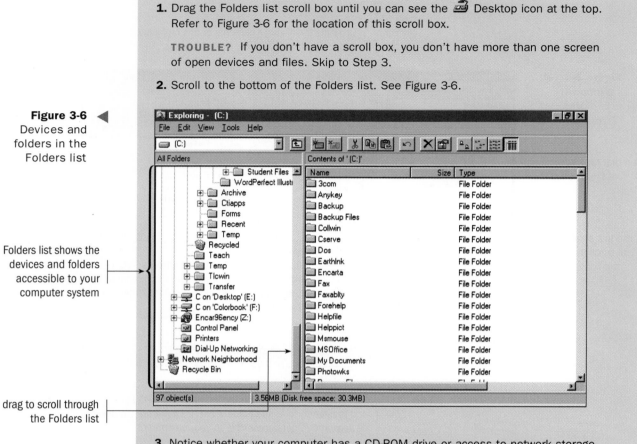

3. Notice whether your computer has a CD-ROM drive or access to network storage devices.

   TROUBLE? Although the computer Bernard is using, shown in Figure 3-6, has both a CD-ROM drive and network disk drive, your list is probably different.

4. After you look at the list of devices and folders, scroll back to the top of the Folders list so you can see the Desktop icon at the top of the list.

Viewing the Folders on a Disk Drive

Like a file cabinet, a typical storage device on your computer contains files and folders. These folders can contain additional files and one or more levels of subfolders. If Explorer displayed all your computer's storage devices, folders, and files at once, it could be a very long list. Instead, Explorer allows you to open devices and folders only when you want to see what they contain. Otherwise, you can keep them closed.

As you've seen, the small icon next to each object in the list, called the device icon or folder icon, represents the device or folder in the Folders list. Many of these icons also have a plus box or minus box next to them that indicates whether the device or folder contains additional folders. Both the device/folder icon and the plus/minus box are controls that you can click to change the display in the Explorer window. You click the plus box to display folders or subfolders, and you click the minus box to hide them. You click the device/folder icon to control the display in the Contents list.

Figure 3-7 explains how each of these controls accomplishes a different task to change the view in the Folders and Contents lists. With practice you'll see how to use these controls to display only what you want.

3.1 NOTE

File Manager showed a separate window for each storage device. With Windows Explorer, you can see all the devices in a single list.

click device icon to display files and folders in Contents list. Double-click device icon to display files and folders in Folders list and contents in Contents list

Figure 3-7 ◀
Controls

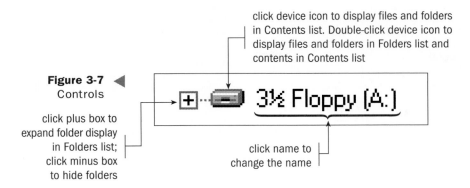

click plus box to expand folder display in Folders list; click minus box to hide folders

click name to change the name

The 3½ Floppy (A:) device icon 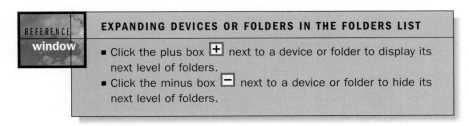 shown in Figure 3-7 might appear with a different name on your computer. This is the icon representing the device that contains your Student Disk. In the Steps in this tutorial, this icon is called simply **drive A**.

You begin assisting Bernard by showing him how you've structured the folders on drive A. You explain to him how the plus/minus box displays or hides the folders on drive A.

REFERENCE **window**

EXPANDING DEVICES OR FOLDERS IN THE FOLDERS LIST

- Click the plus box ⊞ next to a device or folder to display its next level of folders.
- Click the minus box ⊟ next to a device or folder to hide its next level of folders.

To display and hide the levels of folders on drive A:

1. Click ⊞ in front of 🖫 drive A. The folders in the root directory of drive A appear and the plus box in front of drive A changes to a minus box. See Figure 3-8.

   TROUBLE? If you initially see a minus box in front of the device icon for drive A, your drive A folders are already visible in the Folders list. You don't need to click the icon in Step 1.

Figure 3-8 ◀
Folders on drive A

plus/minus box for drive A

plus box indicates Clients folder contains subfolders

folders on drive A

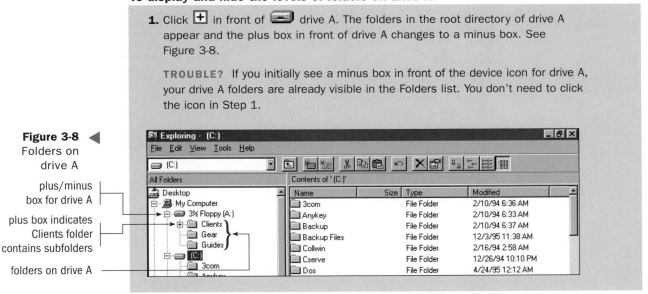

2. Click ⊟ in front of drive A. Now the Folders list shows only drive A, without the folders it contains.

3. Click ⊞ in front of drive A one more time.

When you click the plus box ⊞ next to drive A, you do not necessarily see all the folders on the drive. You only see the first level of folders. If one of these folders contains subfolders, a plus box appears next to it. The Clients folder on drive A has a plus box next to it, indicating that it contains subfolders. When you originally created the structure for Bernard's disk, you grouped his clients into Advanced and Basic, and then grouped the Advanced clients by their primary interests—Alpine, Ice, and Sport.

To view the subfolders for Clients:

1. Click ⊞ next to the Clients folder. You see that Clients contains two subfolders: Advanced and Basic.

2. Click ⊞ next to the Advanced folder. Now you see three additional subfolders: Alpine, Ice, and Sport. See Figure 3-9.

Figure 3-9
Entire folder and subfolder structure on drive A

click minus box to hide subfolders

subfolders of Clients folder

subfolders of Advanced folder

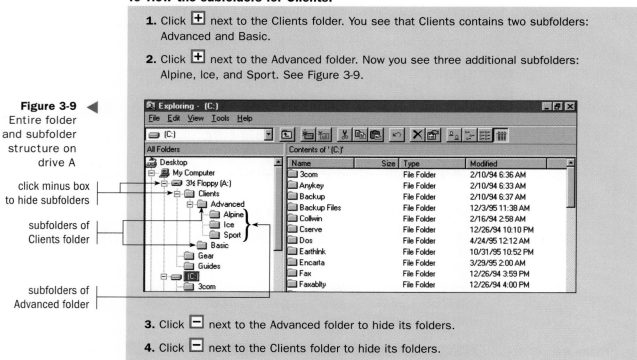

3. Click ⊟ next to the Advanced folder to hide its folders.

4. Click ⊟ next to the Clients folder to hide its folders.

Selecting a Device or Folder

To work with a device or folder, you first click it to select it, and Windows highlights it. It is important to understand that using the plus/minus box does not select a device or folder. To select a device or folder, you must click its *icon*, not its plus/minus box. When you select a device or folder, it becomes active. The **active** device or folder is the one the computer uses when you take an action.

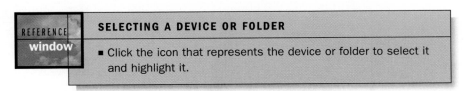

REFERENCE
window

SELECTING A DEVICE OR FOLDER

■ Click the icon that represents the device or folder to select it and highlight it.

For example, if you want to create a new folder on drive A, you first need to select drive A. It then becomes the active drive. If you don't first activate drive A, the new folder you create would be placed in whatever device or folder was currently active—it could be a folder on the hard drive or network drive. How do you know which device or folder is active? Two ways. First, it is highlighted. Second, its name appears at the top of the Contents list and in the title bar, as shown in Figure 3-10.

name of active device
appears at top of Contents
list and in title bar

Figure 3-10
Active device

active device
is highlighted

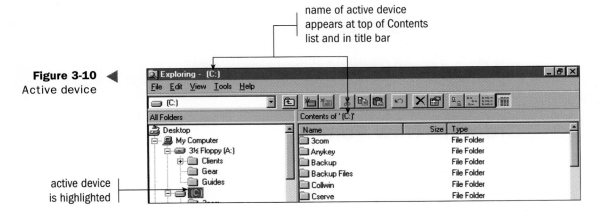

You can experiment with changing the active device and folder by selecting drive A and then selecting the Clients folder.

To select devices and folders:

1. Click ▭ **drive A**. To show that drive A is selected, the computer highlights the label, usually "3½ Floppy (A:)," and displays it in both the title bar and at the top of the Contents list. See Figure 3-11 on the next page.

name of active device
in title bar and
top of contents list

Figure 3-11 ◄
Drive A is the
active device

click drive A device
icon to activate it

Exploring - 3½ Floppy (A:)

File　Edit　View　Tools　Help

3½ Floppy (A:)

All Folders

Contents of '3½ Floppy (A:)'		
Name	Size	Type
Clients		File Folder
Gear		File Folder
Guides		File Folder
Logo	79KB	Bitmap Image
Harness	15KB	Microsoft Excel Worksheet
Rope4	16KB	Microsoft Excel Worksheet
Schedule	20KB	Microsoft Excel Worksheet
Wall	48KB	Microsoft PowerPoint Presentation
Beckman	1KB	Text Document
Chan	1KB	Text Document
Donaldson	1KB	Text Document
Dupree	1KB	Text Document
Fuller	1KB	Text Document
Holmes	1KB	Text Document
Morris	1KB	Text Document
Ngo	1KB	Text Document
Reeve	1KB	Text Document
Sanchez	1KB	Text Document

All Folders:
Desktop
My Computer
3½ Floppy (A:)
Clients
Gear
Guides
(C:)
3com
Anykey
Backup
Backup Files
Collwin
Cserve
Dos
Earthlnk
Encarta
Fax
Faxablty
Forehelp
Helpfile
Helpnist

19 object(s)　　177KB [Disk free space: 1.10MB]

2. Click 📁 **Clients**. The computer highlights the label "Clients" and displays it in the title bar and at the top of the Contents list.

Creating New Folders

Bernard tracks gear usage for both ropes and harnesses. Climbers wear harnesses to attach themselves to the rope for protection in case they fall, and Bernard owns a number of harnesses that his clients use on guided climbs. There is already a folder named "Gear" that contains files for each of the KCS ropes. You decide to create two new subfolders within the Gear folder: one for all files having to do with harnesses, and the other for the ropes files.

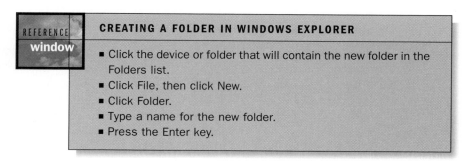

REFERENCE
window

CREATING A FOLDER IN WINDOWS EXPLORER

- Click the device or folder that will contain the new folder in the Folders list.
- Click File, then click New.
- Click Folder.
- Type a name for the new folder.
- Press the Enter key.

The Clients folder is currently active. If you create a new folder now, it will become a subfolder of Clients. Because you want to create the two subfolders in the Gear folder, you must make the Gear folder active.

To create the new Gear subfolders on Bernard's disk:

1. Click 🗀 **Gear** in the Folders list to activate the Gear folder.

   TROUBLE? If you clicked ⊞ instead of the folder icon 🗀 you did not activate the folder. Be sure you click the folder icon. The Gear folder should appear highlighted and the icon should change to 🗁.

2. Click **File** to open the File menu, point to **New**, then click **Folder**. A folder icon labeled "New Folder" appears at the end of the Contents list.

3. Type **Harnesses** as the title of the new folder.

4. Press the **Enter** key. Now create the second subfolder of the Gear folder for all the rope files.

5. Click **File**, point to **New**, click **Folder**, type **Ropes** as the name of the second folder, then press the **Enter** key.

6. Click ⊞ next to the Gear folder to see the new folders in the Folders list. See Figure 3-12.

Figure 3-12 ◀
Creating
new folders

new folders
in Folders list

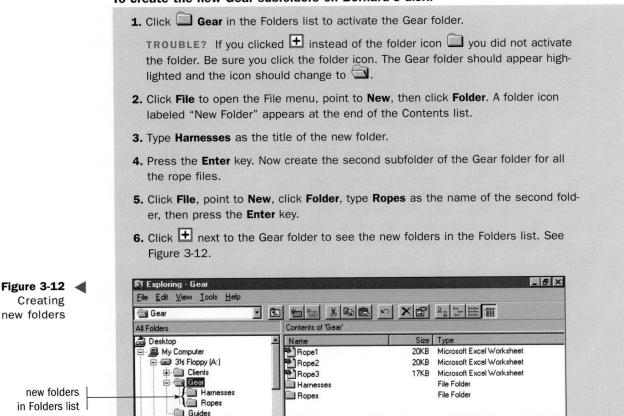

Renaming a Folder

As you and Bernard talk over the current folder structure, you realize that a complete inventory of the KCS gear includes not just ropes and harnesses but many other types of equipment: carabiners, belay plates, chalk bags, runners, and so on. Therefore, the two of you decide to rename the Harnesses folder as "Equipment," so you can store files on just the ropes in the Ropes folder and files for all the other gear in the Equipment folder.

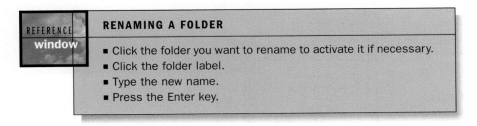

REFERENCE
window

RENAMING A FOLDER

- Click the folder you want to rename to activate it if necessary.
- Click the folder label.
- Type the new name.
- Press the Enter key.

3.1 NOTE

In Explorer you can rename a folder by simply clicking its label, rather than having to use a menu command.

The easiest way to rename a folder is to select the folder, click the folder label (not the plus/minus box or the folder icon), then type the new name.

To change the name of the Harnesses folder to "Equipment":

1. Click 📁 **Harnesses**.

2. Click the *label* **Harnesses**. After a short pause, a flashing insertion point appears at the end of the folder name.

3. Type **Equipment** as the new folder name.

4. Press the **Enter** key.

Adjusting the Width of the Folders List

As you create or view more and more levels of folders, the space for the Folders list might not be wide enough to display all the levels of folders. As a result, you might not be able to see all the device and folder icons. Whether or not this occurs depends on how long your folder names are and how wide the Folders list was in the first place. You can increase the width of the Folders list by dragging the dividing bar that separates the Folders list from the Contents list.

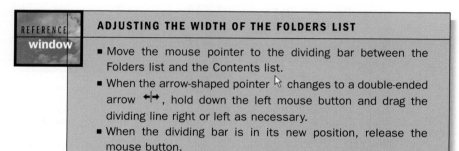

REFERENCE window

ADJUSTING THE WIDTH OF THE FOLDERS LIST

- Move the mouse pointer to the dividing bar between the Folders list and the Contents list.
- When the arrow-shaped pointer ⬚ changes to a double-ended arrow ◄║►, hold down the left mouse button and drag the dividing line right or left as necessary.
- When the dividing bar is in its new position, release the mouse button.

To increase the width of the Folders list:

1. Move the mouse pointer to the dividing bar between the Folders list and the Contents list. The ⬚ pointer changes to a ◄║► pointer.

2. Hold down the left mouse button while you drag the dividing bar to the right about one-half inch, as shown in Figure 3-13.

Figure 3-13 ◄
Adjusting the width of the Windows Explorer lists

double-ended arrow appears when you point at dividing bar

gray bar shows new location as you drag

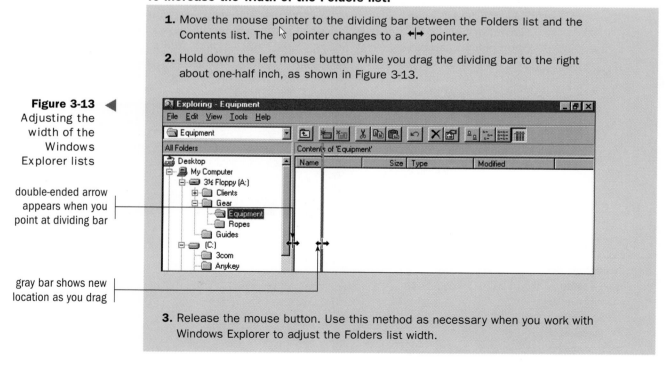

3. Release the mouse button. Use this method as necessary when you work with Windows Explorer to adjust the Folders list width.

Closing Windows Explorer

You have now properly restructured the folders on Bernard's disk. In the next session, you will work with the files on his disk. You can close Windows Explorer by using the Close button on the Exploring window.

To close Windows Explorer:

1. Click the **Close** button ☒ to close the Exploring window. You return to the Windows 95 desktop.

Quick Check

1. _____ is an alternative to using My Computer for file management tasks.

2. The Exploring window is divided into two parts: the _____ list and the _____ list.

3. True or false: If you see folders with the same names on both the right and left sides of the Exploring window, the folders are duplicates and you should erase those on the right side of the screen.

4. True or false: The Folders list displays all the files in a folder.

5. A folder that is contained in another folder is referred to as a(n) _____.

6. You click the _____ to expand the display of folders in the Folders list.

7. If you want to create a new folder on drive A, what should you click in the Folders list?

8. True or false: To adjust the width of the Folders list, be sure the mouse pointer looks like ⇱ before you start to drag the dividing bar.

SESSION

3.2

In Session 3.2 you will work with the right side of the Exploring window, which displays folders and files. You will learn how to switch between icon views and list views of the files, and how to arrange files by name, date, size, and file type. You will also learn how to select multiple files. These skills will help you find, move, copy, and delete files in the process of organizing your disks.

Viewing the Explorer Toolbar

To continue, you need to restart Windows Explorer. Windows Explorer has a toolbar that provides quick access to many Explorer commands. You will use the toolbar shortly, so you should make sure the toolbar is displayed on your screen.

To display the Explorer toolbar:

1. Make sure your Student Disk is in drive A, then start Windows Explorer and scroll the Folders list, if necessary, so you can see drive A.

2. Maximize the Exploring window if necessary.

3. Check your screen to see if the Explorer toolbar is displayed. See Figure 3-14.

4. If the toolbar is not visible on the screen, click **View** on the menu bar, then click **Toolbar** to display it. Figure 3-14 shows the Explorer toolbar.

Figure 3-14 ◄
Explorer toolbar

Explorer toolbar ⟶

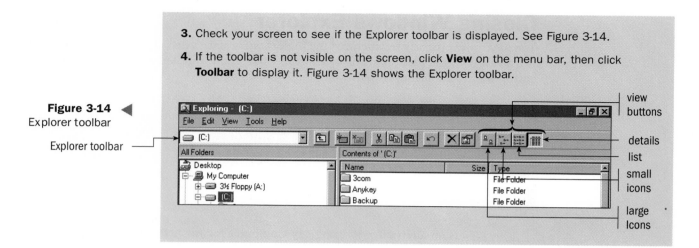

If you forget the function of a toolbar button, you can always point to the button. After a short pause a ToolTip will appear, telling you what the button does.

Viewing the Contents List

The right side of the Exploring window shows the Contents list, which lists the contents, both folders and files, of the active device or folder. Clicking a plus/minus box does not affect the Contents list. To change the Contents list, you must activate a device or folder by clicking its corresponding device or folder icon. Explorer highlights the icon, and the Contents list changes to display the contents of the device or folder you clicked.

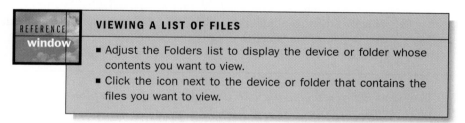

REFERENCE window	**VIEWING A LIST OF FILES**
	▪ Adjust the Folders list to display the device or folder whose contents you want to view.
	▪ Click the icon next to the device or folder that contains the files you want to view.

You and Bernard now examine the contents of drive A.

To view the contents of drive A:

1. Click [icon] **drive A** in the Folders list. See Figure 3-15 if you have trouble locating this icon. The Contents list changes to show the contents of drive A.

   TROUBLE? If nothing happened in your Contents list, it probably already showed the contents of drive A. If this is true, the label at the top of the Contents list will read "Contents of '3½ Floppy (A:)'." Continue to Step 2.

2. Click **View**, then click **Details** so that your Contents list looks like the one in Figure 3-15.

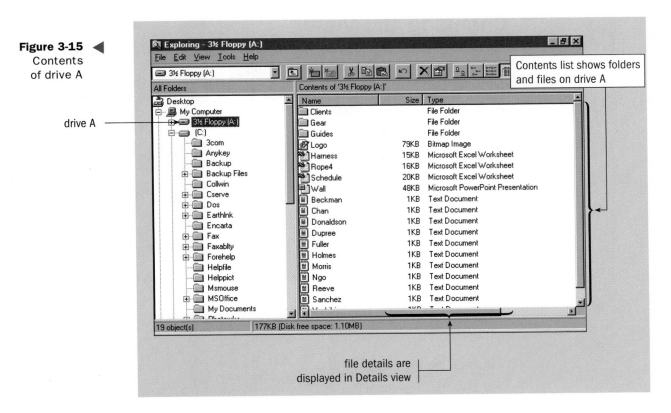

Figure 3-15 ◀
Contents
of drive A

drive A

You can see that the root directory of drive A contains three folders and a number of files; however, you cannot see the contents of the folders in this list. To see the contents of a folder, you must select the folder by clicking it. When the Steps tell you to click a folder icon, click it in the Folders list and not in the Contents list. You want to view the contents of the Gear folder.

To view folder contents:

1. Click ⊞ in front of drive A to display its folders.

2. Click 📁 **Gear** (not the plus box) in the Folders list. The Contents list on the right side of the window changes to display the files in the Gear folder. In addition to the two subfolders you created earlier, there are three files, one for each rope KCS owns. See Figure 3-16.

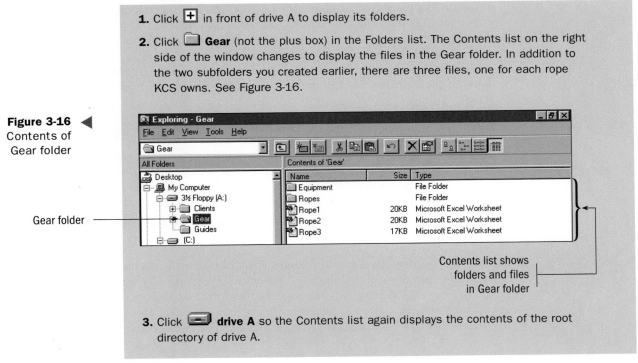

Figure 3-16 ◀
Contents of
Gear folder

Gear folder

3. Click 💾 **drive A** so the Contents list again displays the contents of the root directory of drive A.

Changing the View

Explorer provides four different view options for the Contents list: Large Icons, Small Icons, List, and Details, similar to the view options available in My Computer. Most users prefer to use the Details view because it shows the file size and the date when the file was created or last modified. This information is often useful when making decisions about which files to move and delete.

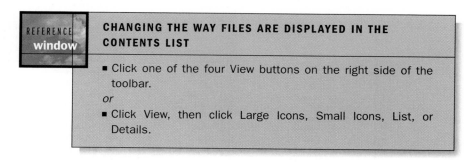

REFERENCE **window**

CHANGING THE WAY FILES ARE DISPLAYED IN THE CONTENTS LIST

- Click one of the four View buttons on the right side of the toolbar.

or

- Click View, then click Large Icons, Small Icons, List, or Details.

You can use the four buttons on the right side of the toolbar to change the way the files are displayed in the Contents list.

To change the file display:

1. Click the **Large Icons** button ⬚ to view the files as large icons.
2. Click the **Small Icons** button ⬚ to view the files as small icons.
3. Click the **List** button ⬚ to view the files as a list.
4. Click the **Details** button ⬚ to view all file details.

Arranging Files in the Contents List

For many file management tasks, one of your first Steps is to locate one or more files that you want to delete, copy, or move. To help you locate files, Explorer provides you with the option to arrange files by name, size, date, or type. The arrangement you use will depend on the file management task you are doing. For example, arranging files by name is useful if you are looking for a particular file to move, copy, or delete and you know its name. If there are any folders in the Contents list, Explorer displays those first.

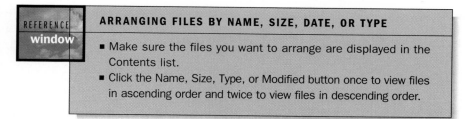

REFERENCE **window**

ARRANGING FILES BY NAME, SIZE, DATE, OR TYPE

- Make sure the files you want to arrange are displayed in the Contents list.
- Click the Name, Size, Type, or Modified button once to view files in ascending order and twice to view files in descending order.

When you view the files in the Contents list using the Details button, a button appears at the top of each of the four columns: Name, Size, Type, and Modified, as shown in Figure 3-17. You can click the button to arrange the files by the corresponding column. For example, clicking the Name button arranges the files by name in ascending order (from A to Z). If you click the Name button a second time, the files appear in descending order (from Z to A).

To arrange the files by name:

1. Click the **Name** button. See Figure 3-17.

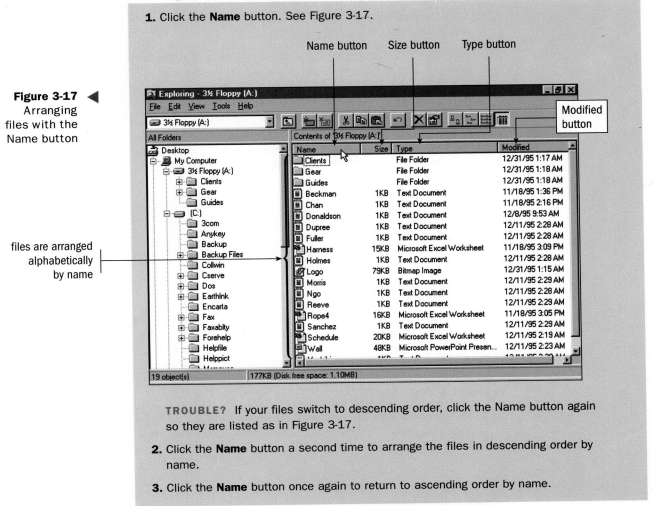

Name button   Size button   Type button

Modified button

Figure 3-17 ◄
Arranging
files with the
Name button

files are arranged
alphabetically
by name

TROUBLE? If your files switch to descending order, click the Name button again so they are listed as in Figure 3-17.

2. Click the **Name** button a second time to arrange the files in descending order by name.

3. Click the **Name** button once again to return to ascending order by name.

Clicking the Size button displays the files in order according to the number of bytes or characters each contains. This is helpful when you need to make more space available on a disk and are trying to decide which files to delete or move to another disk. When the files are arranged in descending order by size, the largest files appear at the top. You can delete those first when you need more disk space.

To arrange the files by size:

1. Click the **Size** button to arrange the files in ascending order by size.

2. Click the **Size** button a second time to arrange the files in descending order by size. The Logo file is the largest file on the disk.

Clicking the Modified button displays the files in order by the date they were modified. This arrangement is useful, for example, if you are looking for a file you know you created yesterday but whose name you have forgotten.

To arrange the files by date:

1. Click the **Modified** button. The files are now listed with the newest or most recently modified file at the top of the list.

   TROUBLE? Depending on the width of the columns in the Contents list, you might have to scroll to the right to see the Modified button.

Sometimes you want to locate all files of a particular type. For example, you might want to quickly locate all the files created with WordPad. This sorting arrangement is useful when you know you created a file using a particular application. Explorer identifies the application that created the file in the Type column.

To arrange the files by type:

1. Click the **Type** button. Explorer now groups the files by application type.

2. Click the **Name** button to restore ascending alphabetical order.

Selecting Files

After you locate the file or files you need for a file management task, you have to tell Explorer which specific file(s) you want to work with. If you want to delete, move or copy a single file, you must first select the file. Take a moment to learn some file selection techniques before working with the files on Bernard's disk.

To select a single file:

1. Click the **Beckman** file to select it. As shown in Figure 3-18, the file is highlighted to show that it is selected, and the status bar indicates that one object is selected (170 bytes in size).

Figure 3-18 ◀
Selecting a
single file

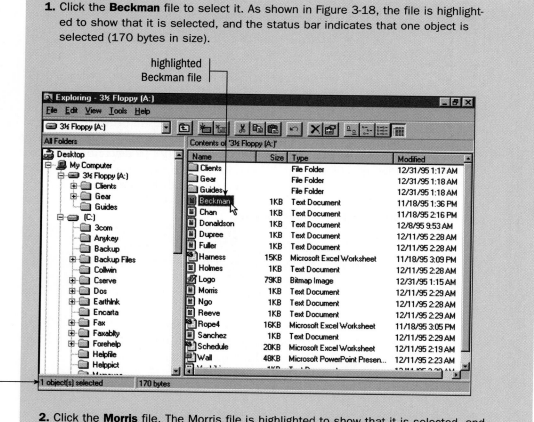

highlighted
Beckman file

Status bar shows that
one object is selected

2. Click the **Morris** file. The Morris file is highlighted to show that it is selected, and Beckman is no longer highlighted.

You can select all the files and folders in a folder or device in a single Step.

To select all files and folders on drive A:

1. Click **Edit**, then click **Select All**. Explorer highlights the files and folders to show they are selected. The status bar now tells you that 19 objects are selected. See Figure 3-19.

Figure 3-19 ◄
Selecting
all files

all files in drive A
(including folders)
are selected

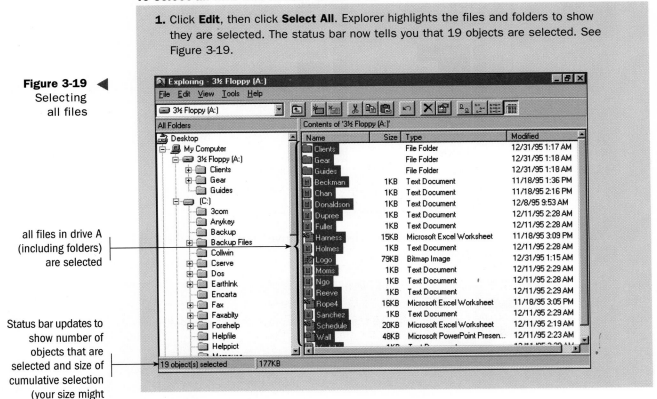

Status bar updates to
show number of
objects that are
selected and size of
cumulative selection
(your size might
be different)

What if you decide that you don't really want everything selected? You can always deselect the objects you have selected by clicking any blank area in the Contents list window.

To deselect the range of files:

1. Click any blank area in the Contents list. The highlighting is removed from all the files to indicate that none are currently selected.

What if you want to work with more than one file, but not all the files in a folder? For example, suppose Bernard wants to delete three of the files in a folder. In Explorer there are two ways to select a group of files. You can select files listed consecutively or you can select files scattered throughout the Contents list. Figure 3-20 on the next page explains the two different ways to select a group of files.

Figure 3-20 ◄
Two ways
to select a
group of files

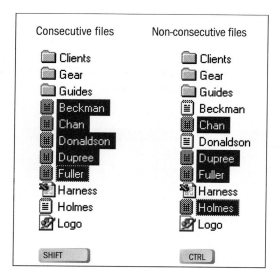

The Shift key lets you select consecutive files, whereas the Ctrl key lets you select non-consecutive files.

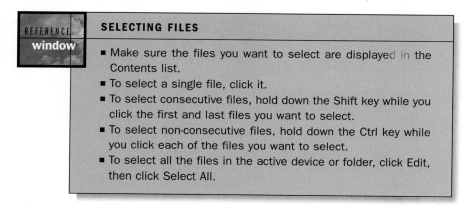

SELECTING FILES

- Make sure the files you want to select are displayed in the Contents list.
- To select a single file, click it.
- To select consecutive files, hold down the Shift key while you click the first and last files you want to select.
- To select non-consecutive files, hold down the Ctrl key while you click each of the files you want to select.
- To select all the files in the active device or folder, click Edit, then click Select All.

You can use the Shift key along with the mouse to select consecutive files. When you are holding down the Shift key, all the files between the first file you click and the second file you click will be selected.

To select consecutive files:

1. Click the **Beckman** file.

2. Hold down the **Shift** key while you click the **Fuller** file. All files from Beckman to Fuller are highlighted. See Figure 3-21.

Figure 3-21 ◄
Selecting
consecutive
files

using the Shift key
and the mouse,
select these
consecutive files

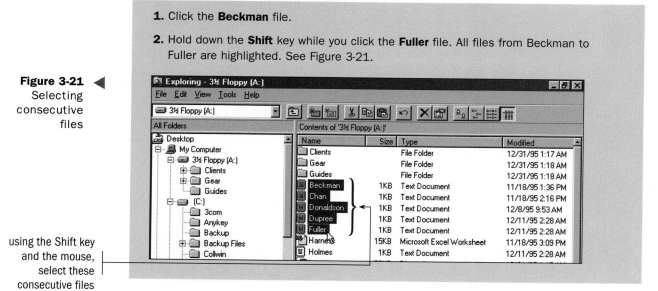

3. Release the **Shift** key.

When you want to select non-consecutive files scattered within a folder, you hold down the Ctrl key while you click the individual files.

To select multiple files using the Ctrl key:

1. Click the **Morris** file. Notice that clicking this file automatically deselects any selected files.

2. Hold down the **Ctrl** key and click the **Reeve** file.

3. Keep holding down the **Ctrl** key and click the **Sanchez** file. All three files should be highlighted. See Figure 3-22.

TROUBLE? If you released the Ctrl key after Step 1, don't worry. Press it again and click Reeve and Sanchez.

Figure 3-22 ◄
Selecting non-consecutive files

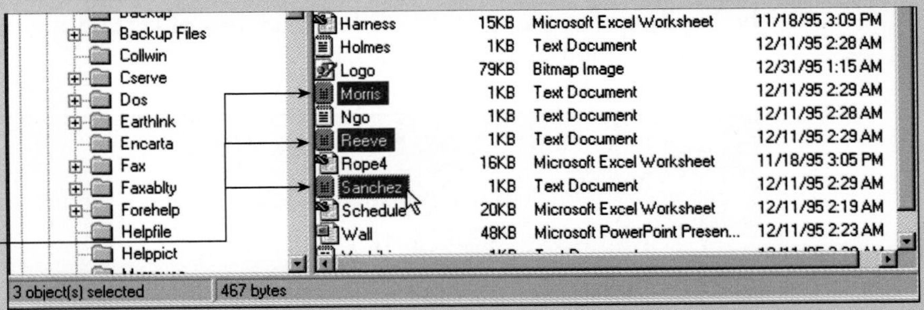

using the Ctrl key and the mouse, select these non-consecutive files

Backup	Harness	15KB	Microsoft Excel Worksheet	11/18/95 3:09 PM
Backup Files	Holmes	1KB	Text Document	12/11/95 2:28 AM
Collwin	Logo	79KB	Bitmap Image	12/31/95 1:15 AM
Cserve	Morris	1KB	Text Document	12/11/95 2:29 AM
Dos	Ngo	1KB	Text Document	12/11/95 2:28 AM
Earthlink	Reeve	1KB	Text Document	12/11/95 2:29 AM
Encarta	Rope4	16KB	Microsoft Excel Worksheet	11/18/95 3:05 PM
Fax	Sanchez	1KB	Text Document	12/11/95 2:29 AM
Faxablty	Schedule	20KB	Microsoft Excel Worksheet	12/11/95 2:19 AM
Forehelp	Wall	48KB	Microsoft PowerPoint Presen...	12/11/95 2:23 AM
Helpfile				
Helppict				

3 object(s) selected   467 bytes

4. Release the **Ctrl** key.

While selecting multiple files with the Ctrl key, you can deselect any file by clicking it again. You can also select more files by holding down the Ctrl key again, then selecting the additional files.

To select and deselect additional files:

1. Hold down the **Ctrl** key and click the **Chan** file to select it. Four files are now selected.

2. Keep holding down the **Ctrl** key and click the **Sanchez** file to deselect it. Now three files are selected: Chan, Morris, and Reeve.

Suppose you want to select all the files *except one* in a folder? You can use the Invert Selection menu option to select all the files that are *not* highlighted.

REFERENCE
window

SELECTING ALL FILES EXCEPT CERTAIN ONES

■ Select the file or files that you do *not* want selected. You can use the Shift or Control keys to select multiple files.
■ Click Edit, then click Invert Selection.

To use Invert Selection to select all files except Dupree:

1. Click the **Dupree** file to select it.

2. Click **Edit**, then click **Invert Selection**. All the files *except* Dupree are now selected.

3. Click a blank area to remove the highlighting for all the files on drive A.

Printing the Exploring Window

You are almost ready to move the new files Bernard created from the root directory into the appropriate folders. Bernard would like to mark the files that need to be moved. He wonders if there's a quick way to get a hard copy (that is, a paper copy) of the Exploring window that he can write on. You tell him that you can temporarily store an image of the Exploring window in memory using the Print Screen key. Then, you can start the WordPad program and paste the Exploring image into a blank WordPad document. Finally, you can print the document (which now contains the Exploring window). It can be handy to have a printout of the structures of certain important devices for reference, so this is a good procedure to learn.

REFERENCE window

PRINTING THE EXPLORING WINDOW

- Adjust the Exploring window so you see the files and folders you want on the printout.
- Press the Print Screen key.
- Click the Start button, click Accessories, then click WordPad.
- Type your name, date, or any other text you want on the print-out of the Exploring window.
- Click Edit, then click Paste to paste the Exploring image into WordPad.
- Click File, then click Print to display the Print dialog box.
- Click OK to print the document.
- Close WordPad, clicking No when asked if you want to save. It is not necessary to save the document you just printed.

The Exploring window is a graphical image, so it can take a fairly long time to print, especially on a dot-matrix printer. If your lab has a dot matrix printer, make sure you pre-view before you print so you do not have to print multiple copies.

To print the Exploring window:

1. Click ⊞ next to Clients, Advanced, and Gear so that all the folders and subfolders on Bernard's disk are visible.

2. Press the **Print Screen** key. Although it seems as if nothing happened, an image of the Exploring window was stored in memory.

3. Click the **Start** button [Start], point to **Programs**, point to **Accessories**, then click **WordPad**. The WordPad window opens.

4. Maximize the WordPad window, type **Bernard Kolbe, 8/22/97** at the top of the WordPad window, then press the **Enter** key twice.

5. Click **Edit**, click **Paste**, then scroll to the top of the document. The Exploring screen image appears in the WordPad document. See Figure 3-23.

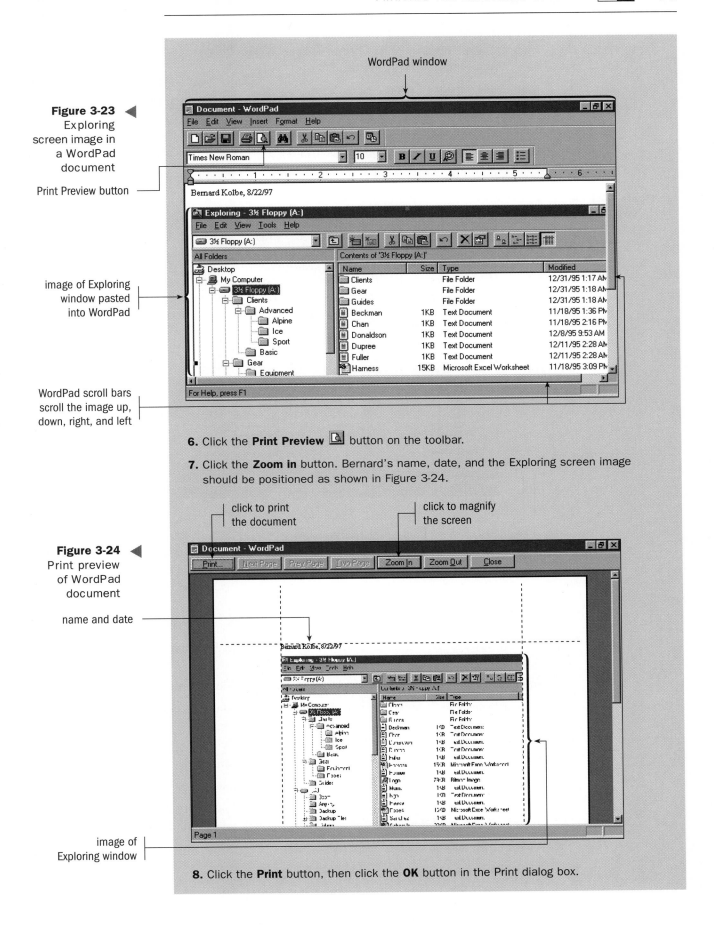

Figure 3-23 ◀
Exploring
screen image in
a WordPad
document

Print Preview button

image of Exploring
window pasted
into WordPad

WordPad scroll bars
scroll the image up,
down, right, and left

6. Click the **Print Preview** 🔍 button on the toolbar.

7. Click the **Zoom in** button. Bernard's name, date, and the Exploring screen image should be positioned as shown in Figure 3-24.

click to print
the document

click to magnify
the screen

Figure 3-24 ◀
Print preview
of WordPad
document

name and date

image of
Exploring window

8. Click the **Print** button, then click the **OK** button in the Print dialog box.

9. Close the WordPad window. When you see a message asking if you want to save the document, click the **No** button.

10. Close Windows Explorer.

Bernard annotates the printout, shown in Figure 3-25, so you know where to move the files in the root directory. You decide to take a break and finish working with Bernard's files tomorrow.

Figure 3-25 ◀
Bernard's
printout

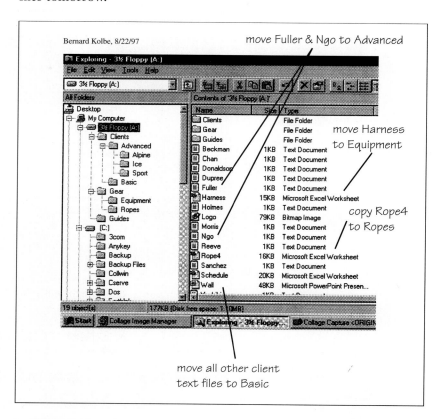

Quick Check

1. True or False: If you click ➕ next to the Clients folder, Explorer displays a list of files in the Clients folder.

2. You click the _____ to display a device's or folder's contents in the Contents list.

3. True or false: The Explorer toolbar contains buttons you use to select consecutive files in the Contents list.

4. Most Windows 95 users prefer to use the _____ view because it shows the file size and the date when the file was created or last modified.

5. The Arrange Icons menu gives you the option to sort files by ____, _____, _____, or _____.

6. If you hold down the _____ key when you select files, you will select consecutive files, whereas if you hold down the _____ key you will select non-consecutive files.

7. What button do you click to view files by date?

8. What happens when you press the Print Screen key?

So far in this tutorial you have learned how to use the Folders list to view the structure of folders on a disk. You have also learned how to view and select files in the Contents list. In Session 3.3, you put these skills to use in the procedures for copying, moving, and deleting files or folders.

Moving a Single File Between Folders

To organize his disk, Bernard needs to move a number of files to different folders. The basic procedure for moving a file is to open the folder that contains the file, select the file, and use the *right* mouse button to drag the file to its new location.

MOVING ONE OR MORE FILES BETWEEN FOLDERS

- Make sure the Contents list shows the files you want to move and the Folders list shows the folders to which you want to move the file(s).
- Click the file(s) you want to move. For multiple files, you can use the Shift or Ctrl keys when you select the files to be moved.
- Hold down the *right* mouse button while you drag the file(s) to the new location.
- Make sure the new location is highlighted before you release the mouse button.
- Click Move Here from the menu.

Bernard has marked the files you need to move on the printout you created in the previous session. You begin by moving the Harness file from the root directory to the Equipment folder.

To move the Harness file:

1. Start Windows Explorer.

2. Click ⌷ **drive A**, then click ⊞ in front of drive A to display its folders.

3. Click ⊞ next to the Gear folder to display its subfolders.

4. Click the **Harness** file in the Contents list, then hold down the *right* mouse button while you drag **Harness** to the Equipment folder as shown in Figure 3-26 on the next page.

   TROUBLE? Don't worry if the filename is displayed as Harness.xls.

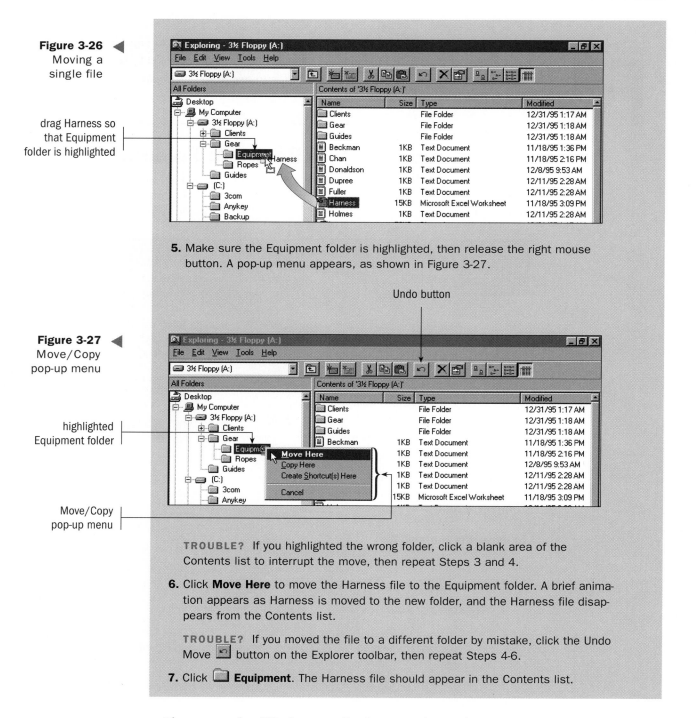

Figure 3-26
Moving a
single file

drag Harness so
that Equipment
folder is highlighted

5. Make sure the Equipment folder is highlighted, then release the right mouse button. A pop-up menu appears, as shown in Figure 3-27.

Undo button

Figure 3-27
Move/Copy
pop-up menu

highlighted
Equipment folder

Move/Copy
pop-up menu

TROUBLE? If you highlighted the wrong folder, click a blank area of the Contents list to interrupt the move, then repeat Steps 3 and 4.

6. Click **Move Here** to move the Harness file to the Equipment folder. A brief animation appears as Harness is moved to the new folder, and the Harness file disappears from the Contents list.

TROUBLE? If you moved the file to a different folder by mistake, click the Undo Move ⟲ button on the Explorer toolbar, then repeat Steps 4-6.

7. Click ▢ **Equipment**. The Harness file should appear in the Contents list.

If you use other Windows applications, you know that in most applications you drag objects with the left mouse button. Although you can drag files in Windows Explorer with the left mouse button, you need to be careful. When you use the left mouse button, Windows Explorer will not open the pop-up menu. Instead, it simply moves or copies the file to the folder you highlight, depending on the circumstances. When you drag a file from one folder to another *on the same drive*, Explorer moves the file. However, when you drag a file from a folder on one drive to a folder *on a different drive*, Explorer copies the file; it does not move it. Therefore, to prevent mistakes, most beginners should use the right mouse button to drag files.

Copying a Single File to a Folder

The procedure for copying a file is similar to the procedure for moving, except that you select Copy Here instead of Move Here from the pop-up menu. Bernard recently purchased a fourth rope, and he is tracking its use in the file Rope4. He wants a copy of the Rope4 file in the Ropes folder.

REFERENCE
window

COPYING ONE OR MORE FILES

- Make sure the folder that contains the file(s) you want to copy is active in the Folders list and the folder to which you want to copy the file(s) is visible.
- Click the file(s) you want to copy. You can use the Shift or Ctrl keys to select more than one file to copy.
- Hold down the *right* mouse button while you drag the file(s) to a new location.
- Make sure the new location is highlighted before you release the mouse button.
- Click Copy Here from the menu.

To copy the Rope4 file into the Ropes folder:

1. Click ⬛ **drive A** to view the files in the root directory once again.

2. Click **Rope4** to select it.

3. Hold down the *right* mouse button while you drag Rope4 to the Ropes folder.

4. Make sure the Ropes folder is highlighted, then release the right mouse button.

5. Click **Copy Here** from the pop-up menu. An animation shows Rope4 being copied from the root directory to the Ropes folder.

   Notice that Rope4 is still displayed in the Contents list for drive A, because you copied the file rather than moved it.

6. Click 🗀 **Ropes** and notice that Rope4 appears in the Contents list for this folder.

Moving or Copying Multiple Files Between Folders

You can move or copy more than one file at a time by selecting multiple files before you drag. Remember that you can use the Ctrl key, the Shift key, or the Select All command on the Edit menu to select more than one file. Bernard wants to move the three rope files from the Gear folder to the Ropes folder. The rope files are listed consecutively, so you should use the Shift key to quickly select these three files before you move them as a group.

To move the rope files to the Ropes folder:

1. Click 🗀 **Gear** to activate the Gear folder and view the other rope files, which also need to be moved into the Ropes folder.

2. Click the **Rope1** file.

3. Hold down the **Shift** key and click the **Rope3** file to select all three rope files.

4. With the pointer over one of the selected files, hold down the *right* mouse button while you drag the selected files to the **Ropes** folder. See Figure 3-28.

Figure 3-28 ◀
Moving a
group of files

outline of the files
you want to move

highlight shows
the destination
for the files

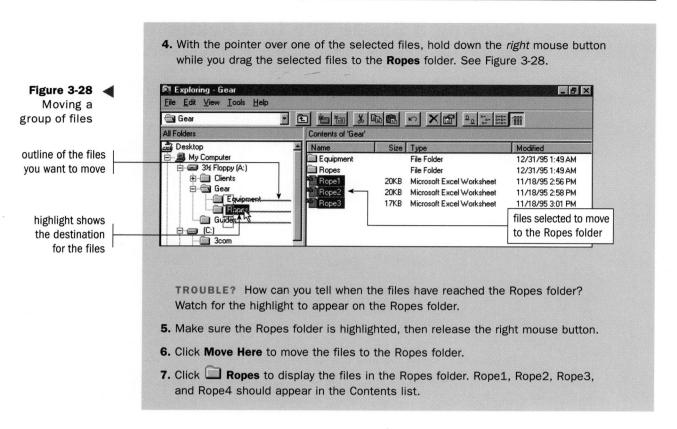

files selected to move
to the Ropes folder

TROUBLE? How can you tell when the files have reached the Ropes folder? Watch for the highlight to appear on the Ropes folder.

5. Make sure the Ropes folder is highlighted, then release the right mouse button.

6. Click **Move Here** to move the files to the Ropes folder.

7. Click ▭ **Ropes** to display the files in the Ropes folder. Rope1, Rope2, Rope3, and Rope4 should appear in the Contents list.

You've got Bernard's gear files organized, so now it's time to look at the new client files he added. Mark Fuller and George Ngo are interested exclusively in alpine climbing, so you decide to move the Fuller and Ngo client files into the Alpine folder.

To move non-consecutive files from one folder to another:

1. Click ▭ **drive A** to display the files it contains in the Contents list, then click ⊞ in front of Clients and Advanced.

2. Click the **Fuller** file.

3. Hold down the **Ctrl** key while you click the **Ngo** file.

4. Release the **Ctrl** key.

5. Drag the files to the Alpine folder using the *right* mouse button.

6. Click **Move Here**.

7. Click ▭ **Alpine**. The Contents list should include the files you just moved, plus the ones that were already there. See Figure 3-29.

Figure 3-29 ◀
Alpine folder
with moved
files

files you moved
from root directory
to Alpine folder

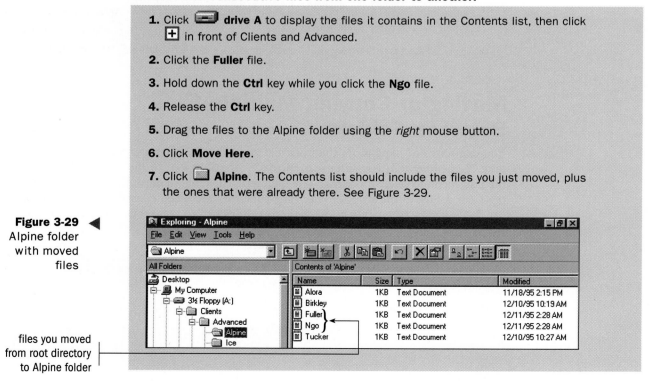

You need to move the remaining client files from the root directory into the Basic folder. You can combine some of the methods you have already learned to complete this task most efficiently. For instance, notice that the client files are all text files. If you arrange these files by type, they'll all be next to each other, so you can select them as a group and drag them together to the Basic folder.

To move a group of related files to a new folder:

1. Click ⬜ **drive A** to view the contents of the root directory.

2. Click the **Type** button. The client text files are now grouped together at the bottom of the Contents list.

   TROUBLE?　The Type button is at the top of the third column in the Contents list.

3. Click the **Beckman** file, hold down the **Shift** key, then click the **Yoshiki** file.

4. Move the client files into the **Basic** folder.

Bernard's disk is now restructured, with the gear and client files in the correct folders.

Moving or Copying Files Between a Floppy Disk and a Hard Disk

In the business world, companies use floppy disks to share files and information with clients and project members; telecommuters (workers who work on both an office computer and a home computer) use floppy disks to take files to and from the office, and software companies distribute programs and files on floppy disks. In your school computer lab, in contrast, you will rarely find yourself in a situation where you need to copy a file from your floppy disk to the hard disk of a lab computer. However, if you have a computer at home, you might want to move or copy files from your floppy disk to your hard disk to take advantage of its speed and large storage capacity.

Moving or copying files from a floppy disk to a hard disk is similar to the procedure for moving or copying files between folders. To practice this task, copy the Excel spreadsheet file named Schedule.xls to the hard disk.

To copy a file from a floppy disk to the hard disk:

1. If necessary, use the scroll bar to position the All Folders list so you can see the icon for drive C.

2. Click ⬜ **drive C** in the Folders list.

3. Click **File**, point to **New**, then click **Folder** to create a new folder on drive C.

   TROUBLE?　If you receive a warning message telling you that you can't create a folder on drive C, you might be on a network that restricts hard-drive access. Ask your instructor or technical support person about other options for working on a hard drive, and read through the rest of this section to learn how you would work on a hard drive if you had the opportunity.

4. Type **Climbing** as the name of the new folder, then press **Enter** to finalize the name.

   TROUBLE?　If there is already a Climbing folder on the hard disk, you must specify a different name. Use the name "Climb" with your initials, such as "ClimbJP." Substitute this folder name for the Climbing folder for the rest of the tutorial.

5. Click ⬜ **drive A** to display its contents in the Contents list.

6. Click the **Schedule** file to select it.

7. Hold down the *right* mouse button while you drag the **Schedule** file to the **Climbing** folder on drive C. See Figure 3-30.

Figure 3-30 ◀
Copying a file
from a floppy
disk to a
hard disk

folder you created
on hard drive

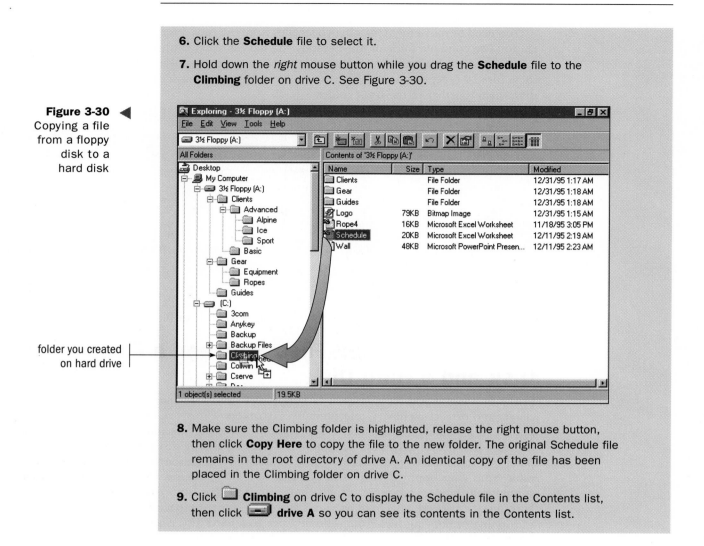

8. Make sure the Climbing folder is highlighted, release the right mouse button, then click **Copy Here** to copy the file to the new folder. The original Schedule file remains in the root directory of drive A. An identical copy of the file has been placed in the Climbing folder on drive C.

9. Click 🗀 **Climbing** on drive C to display the Schedule file in the Contents list, then click 🖳 **drive A** so you can see its contents in the Contents list.

Copying a File From One Floppy Disk to Another Floppy Disk

You notice that Bernard has a PowerPoint file on his disk called Wall; you ask him about it. He explains that he is putting together a slide presentation for civic leaders that proposes building an artificial climbing wall in the area. You tell Bernard that you would love to help him develop the slide show; if he gave you a copy of the file you could work on it on your computer at home. He agrees, but says he doesn't know how to make you a copy because there is only one disk drive on the computer.

If your computer has only one floppy disk drive, you can't just drag a file from one floppy disk to another because you can't put both floppy disks in the drive at the same time. So how do you copy the file from one floppy to another? You first copy the file to a temporary location on the hard drive, then insert the destination floppy disk into drive A and finally move the file from the hard disk to the floppy disk. Figure 3-31 shows how this procedure works.

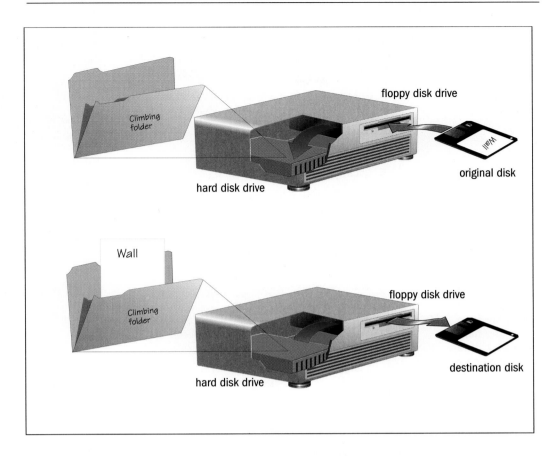

Figure 3-31 ◀
Copying a file
to the hard disk
and then to
a different
floppy disk

To carry out this procedure, you need two disks: your Student Disk and another for-matted floppy disk. You can use the Backup disk you created in Tutorial 2 or any other formatted disk.

REFERENCE window	**COPYING A FILE FROM ONE FLOPPY DISK TO ANOTHER USING A SINGLE FLOPPY DISK DRIVE**

- Make sure you have a folder on the hard drive to which you can copy a file. If necessary, create a new folder on the hard drive.
- Copy the file to the hard drive.
- Take your Student Disk out of the floppy drive and insert the floppy disk on which you want the file copied.
- Click View, then click Refresh to tell the computer you switched disks.
- *Move* the file from the hard disk to the floppy that is now in the floppy disk drive.
- If you created a temporary file on the hard drive, delete it.

To copy one file from your Student Disk to a different floppy disk:

1. Click the **Wall** file to select it.

2. Hold down the *right* mouse button while you drag the **Wall** file to the **Climbing** folder on drive C, release the mouse button when the Climbing folder is high-lighted, then click **Copy Here** to copy the file to drive C.

3. Remove your Student Disk and insert the other formatted floppy disk into drive A.

4. Click **View**, then click **Refresh** to indicate that you switched disks. The Refresh command examines the contents of the disk again and updates the Contents list accordingly.

5. Click the **Climbing** folder on drive C.

6. Click the **Wall** file to select it, then hold down the *right* mouse button while you drag the **Wall** file to drive A. See Figure 3-32.

drag the Wall file from the Climbing folder to the floppy disk in drive A

contents of Climbing folder on the hard drive

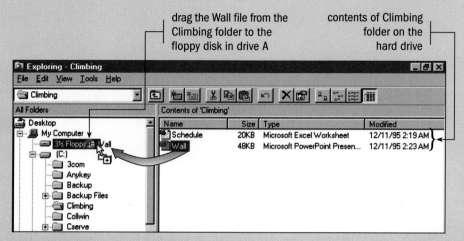

Figure 3-32 ◀ Dragging the Wall file from the hard drive to the floppy disk

7. Release the right mouse button, then click **Move Here** to move the file to drive A.

8. Click drive A and make sure the Wall file is displayed in its Contents list, then remove the floppy disk from drive A.

9. Place your Student Disk back in drive A, click **View**, then click **Refresh** to view the files on the Student Disk.

Deleting Files and Folders

Looking over the Contents list of the drive A root directory of Bernard's disk, you realize that you could delete the Rope4 file since there's a copy of it in the Equipment folder.

When you delete a file or folder from the hard drive, recall that it goes into the Recycle Bin, so if you make a mistake you can always recover the file or folder. Once you delete a file from a floppy disk, though, there is no easy way of recovering it, so be sure before deleting that you are doing the right thing.

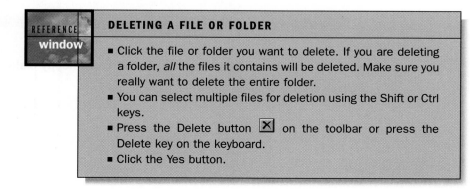

REFERENCE window

DELETING A FILE OR FOLDER

- Click the file or folder you want to delete. If you are deleting a folder, *all* the files it contains will be deleted. Make sure you really want to delete the entire folder.
- You can select multiple files for deletion using the Shift or Ctrl keys.
- Press the Delete button ☒ on the toolbar or press the Delete key on the keyboard.
- Click the Yes button.

To delete the Rope4 file:

> **1.** Make sure the Contents list displays the files in the root directory.
>
> **TROUBLE?** Click [icon] drive A in the Folders list.
>
> **2.** Click **Rope4**.
>
> **3.** Press the **Delete** key, then click the **Yes** button.

Two recent ice-climbing accidents have convinced Bernard to stop offering ice climbing because it's simply too unpredictable and dangerous. This business decision affects the folder structure on Bernard's disk. You decide to move the client files in the Ice folder into the Advanced folder and then delete the Ice folder altogether.

To move the files from Ice to Advanced, then delete the Ice folder:

> **1.** If the folder structure of drive A is no longer displayed in the Folders list, click [+] next to drive A.
>
> **2.** Click [+] next to Clients and Advanced so you can see the Ice folder in the Folders list.
>
> **3.** Click [icon] **Ice**.
>
> **4.** Click **Edit** on the menu bar, then click **Select All** to select the Kranmer and Wei files.
>
> **5.** Drag the selection to the Advanced folder using the *right* mouse button, then click **Move Here**.
>
> **6.** Click [icon] **Ice**.
>
> **7.** Click the **Delete** button [X].
>
> **8.** When you see the message, "Are you sure you want to remove the folder 'Ice' and all its contents?" click the **Yes** button.
>
> **9.** Click [icon] **Advanced** so you can verify that the Kranmer and Wei files have been correctly moved here from the Ice folder.

You've finished organizing Bernard's disk, and as you're getting ready to go, the attendant at the business services center reminds you to be sure to delete any work from the hard drive so it doesn't get cluttered. You should always "clean up" after a session on a computer that doesn't belong to you. You can do so easily by simply removing the Climbing folder from drive C.

To delete the Climbing folder from drive C:

> **1.** Click the **Climbing** folder on drive C, scrolling as necessary to locate it in the Folders list.
>
> **2.** Click the **Delete** button [X] to display the Confirm Folder Delete dialog box. See Figure 3-33 on the next page.

Figure 3-33 ◀
Confirm Folder
Delete
dialog box

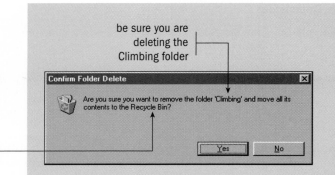

be sure you are
deleting the
Climbing folder

be sure the folder will
go to the Recycle Bin

TROUBLE? If a message appears telling you you can't perform this operation, your system administrator might have restricted deletion privileges from the hard drive. Continue reading the rest of the tutorial.

3. Make sure that the message indicates the Climbing folder will be moved to the Recycle Bin.

TROUBLE? If a different filename appears in the Confirm Folder Delete dialog box, click the No button and go back to Step 1.

4. Click the **Yes** button to delete the folder from drive C.

5. Close Explorer.

Quick Check

1. Why is it wise to use the right mouse button rather than the left to drag files in Windows Explorer?

2. When you take one floppy disk out of the disk drive and put another disk in, you should use the _____ command to tell the computer about the switch.

3. True or False: You can copy a file from one floppy disk to another even if you only have one floppy disk drive in your computer and access to a hard drive.

4. True or False: When you delete a folder, you should first move out any files that you don't want to delete.

5. True or False: When you delete files or folders from the floppy disk, they go into the Recycle Bin.

End Note

You look over the structure of folders and files on Bernard's disk and realize that as his business increases the structure will be increasingly more useful. You've used the power of Windows Explorer to simplify tasks such as locating, moving, copying, and deleting files. You can apply these skills to larger file management challenges when you are using a computer of your own and need to organize and work with the files on your hard drive.

Tutorial Assignments

1. Preparing a File Listing Bernard would like a list of all the gear KCS owns. Use the skills you learned in this tutorial to place all the gear files in the Gear folder, delete the Gear subfolders, and then print out the folder's contents.

    a. Start Windows Explorer, place your Student Disk in drive A, then click the drive A device icon. Open the Gear folder and its subfolders in the Folders list, and then move the rope and harness files from each subfolder into the Gear folder.

    b. Delete the Ropes and Equipment folders.

    c. View the files in the Gear folder by date in descending order (the newest first), then print the Exploring screen using the techniques you learned in this tutorial.

2. Copying Files to the Hard Drive Bernard wants to place his sport-climbing client files on the hard drive to work with them on an advertisement campaign. The Sport folder is a subfolder of Advanced, which is itself a subfolder of Clients.

    a. Create a new folder on drive C called "Advertise."

    b. Copy the client files in the Sport folder on your Student Disk to the Advertise folder on the hard drive.

    c. Open the Advertise folder on the hard drive to display the files it contains.

    d. Print the Exploring screen.

    e. Delete the Advertise folder from the hard drive when your printout is complete.

3. Creating a New Folder and Copying Files Use the Quick Format option to format your Student Disk, then make a new Student Disk. Use the Windows 95 New Perspectives Introductory option on the CTI Windows 95 Applications menu. Bernard now wants a folder that contains all the clients he has because he'd like to do a general mailing to everyone advertising an expedition to the Tetons. (*Hint:* The client files are all text files, so consider viewing the files in the root directory by type. Don't forget that there are also client files in the Client folder and its subfolders.)

    a. Create a folder called "All Clients" on the drive A root directory and copy all the text files into the All Clients folder.

    b. Open the Clients folder and all its subfolders one at a time, and copy the text files from those folders into the new All Clients folder.

    c. Print out the Exploring screen showing the All Clients folder *arranged by name.*

    d. Delete the All Clients folder and all its contents. (*Hint:* You don't have to delete the files one at a time. You can simply click the All Clients folder and use the Delete command.)

4. Restructuring a Disk Use Quick Format to format your Student Disk, then make a new Student Disk. This time use the Windows 95 New Perspectives Brief option on the CTI Windows 95 Applications menu (the files you worked with in Tutorial 2). Rearrange the files on the disk so they correspond to Figure 3-34. Create the new folders shown in Figure 3-34. Delete any files or folders that are not shown in the figure. Print out the Explorer screen that shows your new organization and the files in the Yellowstone Park folder *arranged by size.*

Figure 3-34 ◄

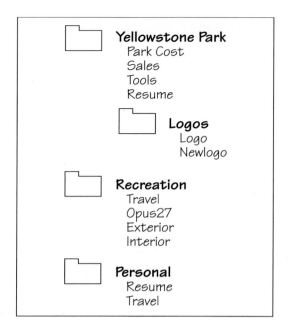

5. Copying Between Floppy Disks Suppose someone who doesn't know how to use the Windows Explorer (she missed class) wants to copy the Guides folder from her Student Disk to another floppy disk. Try this yourself, and as you go through the procedure, write down each Step so this student would be able to follow the Steps and make a copy of Guides without knowing how to use Explorer.

6. Creating a Folder Structure When you complete your computer class, you are likely to use a computer for other courses in your major and for general education requirements such as English and Math. Think about how you would organize the floppy disk that would hold the files for your courses, then prepare a disk to contain your files.
   a. Make a sketch of this organization.
   b. Use Quick Format to erase the contents of your Student Disk.
   c. Create the folder structure on your Student Disk (even though you don't have any files to place in the folders right now). Use subfolders to help sort files for class projects (your composition course, for example, might have a midterm and final paper).
   d. Place an image of the Exploring screen into WordPad using the Print screen key and the methods described in this tutorial.
   e. Use WordPad to write one or two paragraphs explaining your plan. Your explanation should include information about your major, the courses you plan to take, and how you might use computers in those courses.
   f. Print your WordPad document, then close WordPad. You don't need to save this file.

7. Exploring Your Computer's Devices, Folders, and Files Answer each of the following questions about the devices, folders, and files on your lab computers. You can find all the answers using the Exploring window and its menus.
   a. How many folders (not subfolders) are on drive C?
   b. How many of these folders on drive C have subfolders? What is the easiest way to find the answer to this question?
   c. Which folder on drive C contains the most subfolders?

d. Which folder or subfolder on drive C contains the most files? How could you tell?

e. Do you have a Windows folder on drive C? If so, how many objects does it contain?

f. Do you have a DOS folder on your disk? If so, what is the size of the largest file in this folder?

g. Does your computer have a CD-ROM drive? If so, what drive letter is assigned to the CD-ROM?

h. Does your computer have access to a network storage device? If so, indicate the letter(s) of the network storage device(s).

i. How much space on drive C do the files and folders occupy?

8. Separating Program and Data Files Hard-disk management differs from floppy-disk management because a hard disk contains programs and data, whereas a floppy disk (unless it is an installation disk that you got from a software company) generally only contains data files. On a hard disk, a good management practice is to keep programs in folders separate from data files. Keeping this in mind, read the following description, draw a sketch of the folder structure described, then make a sketch of how the current structure could be improved.

The Marquette Chamber of Commerce uses a computer to maintain its membership list and to track dues. It also uses the computer for most correspondence. All the programs and data used by the Chamber of Commerce are on drive C. The membership application software is in a folder called Members. The data file for the membership is in a subfolder of Members called Member Data. The accounting program used to track income and expenditures is in a folder called Accounting Programs. The data for the current year is in a folder directly under the drive C icon called Accounting Data 1997. The accounting data from 1995 and 1996 are stored in two subfolders of the folder called Accounting Programs. The word-processing program is in a folder called Word. The documents created with Word are stored in the Member Data folder. Finally, Windows 95 is stored in a folder called Windows, which has ten subfolders.

Lab Assignments

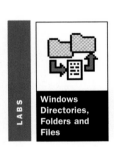

LABS

Windows Directories, Folders and Files

Windows Directories, Folders, and Files Graphical user interfaces such as MacOS, Windows 3.1, and Windows 95 use a filing system metaphor for file management. In this Lab, you will learn the basic concepts of these file system metaphors. With this background, you will find it easy to understand how to manage files with graphical user interfaces.

1. Click the Steps button to learn how to manipulate directories, folders and files. As you proceed through the Steps, answer all of the Quick Check questions that appear. After you complete the Steps, you will see a Quick Check Summary Report. Follow the instructions on the screen to print this report.

2. Click the Explore button. Make sure drive a: is the default drive. Double-click the a:\ folder to display the folder contents, then answer the following questions:

a. How many files are in the root directory of drive a:?

b. Are the files on drive a: data files or program files? How can you tell?

c. Does the root directory of drive a: contain any subdirectories? How can you tell?

3. Make sure you are in Explore. Change to drive c: as the default drive. Double-click the c:\ folder to display its contents, then answer the following questions:

a. How many data files are in the root directory of drive c:?

b. How many program files are in the root directory of drive c:?

c. Does the root directory of drive c: contain any subdirectories? How can you tell?

d. How many files are in the dos folder?

    e. Complete the diagram in Figure 3-35 to show the arrangement of folders on drive c:. Do not include files.

Figure 3-35 ◀

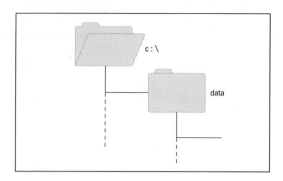

4. Open and close folders, and change drives as necessary to locate the following files. After you find the file, write out its file specification:

    a. config.sys, b.win.ini, c.toolkit.wks, d.meeting.doc

    b. newlogo3.bmp, f.todo.doc

Customizing Windows 95 for Increased Productivity

CASE

Companions, Inc.

Bow Falls, Arizona, is a popular Sun Belt retirement mecca that is at the same time a college town with several distinguished universities and colleges. Beth Yuan, a graduate of Bow Falls University, realized that the unusual mix of the old and young in her town might be perfectly suited to a services business. She formed Companions, Inc. to provide older area residents with trained personal care assistants and to help with housecleaning, home maintenance, and running errands. Beth's company now includes employees who work directly with clients and an office staff that help her manage the day-to-day tasks of running a business. Many of Beth's employees are students at local colleges who like the flexible hours and who enjoy spending time with the elderly residents.

The offices of Companions, Inc. are equipped with computers that maintain client records, schedule employees, manage company finances, develop training materials, and create informational documents about Beth's business. Beth recently upgraded her computers to Windows 95. She has heard that it's easy to change Windows 95 settings to reflect the needs of her office staff. She asks you to find a way to make it easier to access documents and computer resources. She would also like you to give the desktop a corporate look and feel. Finally, she wonders if you can customize Windows 95 to adapt it to users with special needs.

SESSION

4.1

In this session, you will learn how to use the right mouse button to place a Notepad document icon on the desktop and to stamp the document with the time and date. You will create shortcuts to the objects you use most often, including your computer's floppy disk drive, a document, and a printer. You will learn how to use the icons you create and to restore your desktop to its original state.

Right-clicking to Open an Object's Menu

Your mouse device usually has two buttons: one on the left and one on the right. You already know how to use the left mouse button to select an object. You can also click an object with the right mouse button, which is called right-clicking. **Right-clicking** both selects the object and opens a menu that shows the most common commands for that object.

Figure 4-1 ◀
Clicking with
the left and
right mouse
buttons

clicking with left
mouse button
selects object

click with left
mouse button

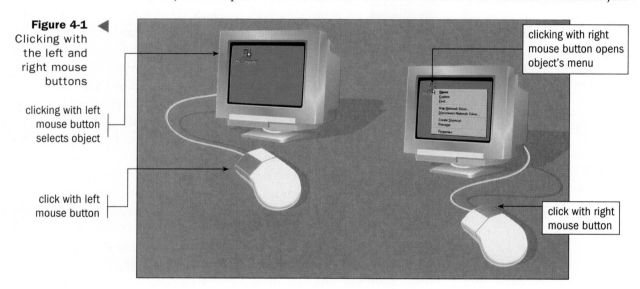

clicking with right
mouse button opens
object's menu

click with right
mouse button

3.1 NOTE

In some Windows 3.1 applications, right-clicking an object opens a menu. In Windows 95, right-clicking has become a standard feature of the operating system so that right-clicking any object opens a menu of common commands and properties.

The left mouse button in Figure 4-1 clicks the My Computer icon to select it. The right mouse button clicks the My Computer icon to open its menu. One of the most important commands on this menu is the Properties command, which gives you access to an object's settings. You'll learn how to use the Properties command in Session 4.2. For now, try opening the My Computer menu by right-clicking its icon.

To open the My Computer menu:

1. Start Windows 95, if necessary.

2. Position the pointer over the My Computer icon.

3. Click the **My Computer** icon with the *right* mouse button. Figure 4-2 shows the menu that opens.

   TROUBLE? If you are using a trackball instead of a mouse there might be a third button in the middle of the device. Be sure you click with the button on the far right.

   TROUBLE? If your menu looks slightly different from the one shown in Figure 4-2, don't worry. Different computers have different commands, depending on their configuration.

Figure 4-2 ◄
Menu that opens when you right-click the My Computer icon

click the My Computer icon with the right mouse button

Properties command accesses an object's properties

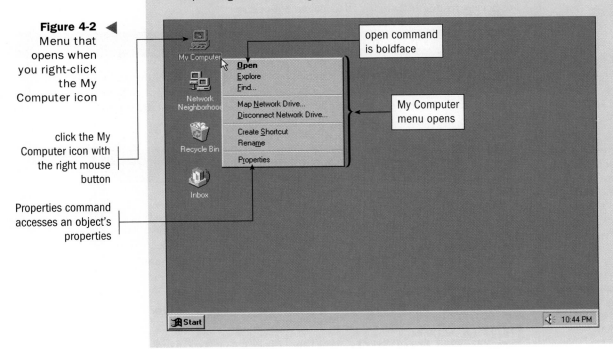

open command is boldface

My Computer menu opens

3.1 NOTE

Right-clicking and then selecting Open accomplishes the same result as double-clicking.

Take a look at the My Computer menu that opens when you right-click. The first command for objects on the desktop is usually Open. Clicking Open on this menu accomplishes the same result as left-clicking the object and pressing Enter. For example, in earlier tutorials you opened My Computer by left-clicking and pressing Enter. The Properties command is usually at the bottom of the menu. You'll use this command later in the tutorial.

In the rest of this tutorial, the steps tell you to "right-click" whenever you need to click with the right mouse button. You can right-click almost anything in Windows 95: a file, a folder, a drive, the taskbar, and even the desktop itself.

To close the My Computer menu:

1. Click an empty area of the desktop with the *left* mouse button to close the My Computer menu.

Document-centric Desktops

Windows 95 automatically places several icons on your desktop, such as the My Computer and the Recycle Bin. You can place additional icons on the desktop that represent objects such as printers, disk drives, programs, and documents. For example, you can create an icon right on your desktop that represents your resume. To open this document, you use its icon. You no longer have to navigate menus or windows or even locate the program you used to create the document. A desktop that gives this kind of immediate access to documents is called **document-centric**.

Creating a Document Icon on the Desktop

Employees in the Companions offices keep a log of their telephone calls using Notepad. The Notepad accessory that comes with Windows 95 includes a **time-date stamp** that automatically inserts the date every time you open the document. Figure 4-3 shows you a Notepad document with automatic time-date stamps.

Figure 4-3 ◄
Notepad document with time-date stamp

time and date automatically inserted each time you open document

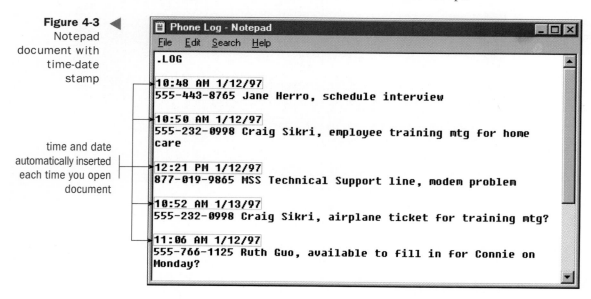

You create a new document on the desktop by right-clicking the desktop and then selecting the type of document you want from a list. An icon, called a **document icon**, appears on the desktop that represents your document.

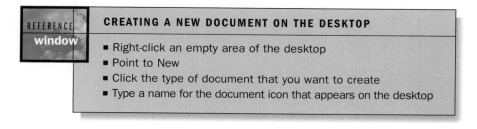

REFERENCE window

CREATING A NEW DOCUMENT ON THE DESKTOP

- Right-click an empty area of the desktop
- Point to New
- Click the type of document that you want to create
- Type a name for the document icon that appears on the desktop

The phone log is a perfect candidate for a document on the desktop because employees use it so frequently. When you use the document icon to open the document, Windows 95 locates and starts the appropriate software program for you. To create a Notepad document, you choose the Text Document option.

To create a Notepad document icon on the desktop:

1. Right-click a blank area of the desktop, then point to **New**. The menu shown in Figure 4-4 opens.

TROUBLE? If no menu appears, you might have clicked with the left mouse button instead of the right. Repeat Step 1.

TROUBLE? If your New menu looks different from the one shown in Figure 4-4, don't worry. The document types that appear on the New menu depend on what software is loaded on your computer.

Figure 4-4 ◀
Creating a new text document

desktop menu opens when you right-click

click to create new text document

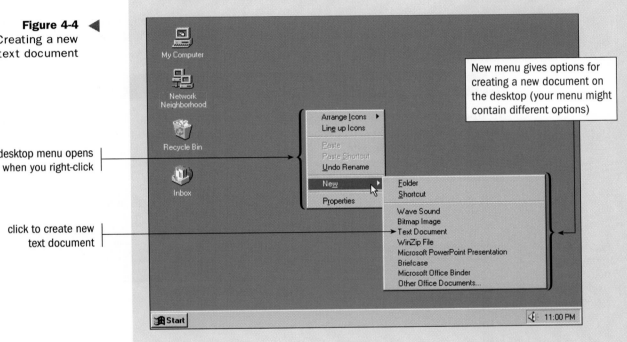

New menu gives options for creating a new document on the desktop (your menu might contain different options)

2. Click **Text Document**. A document icon for your new text document appears on the desktop. See Figure 4-5.

TROUBLE? If you receive an error message when you try to create a new document on the desktop, your school might not allow you to make any changes to the desktop. Ask your instructor which sections of this tutorial your lab allows you to complete.

Figure 4-5 ◀
Document icon

icon represents a text document

type name here

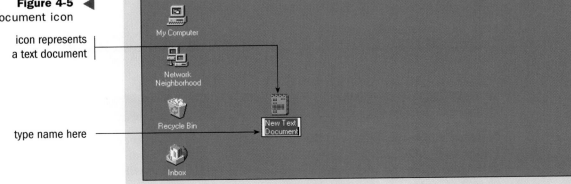

3. Type **Phone Log** as the name of your document.

4. Press the **Enter** key. See Figure 4-6.

TROUBLE? If you see a message about changing the filename extension, click No and type Phone Log.txt.

Figure 4-6 ◀
Phone Log
document icon

new name ——————

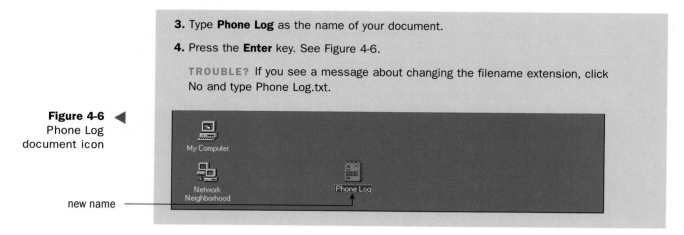

You can often identify an object's type by its icon. The Phone Log document icon identifies a Notepad text document. Later in this tutorial you'll see other icons that represent other object types.

Opening a Document on the Desktop

To open a document on your desktop, you click the document icon and then press the Enter key. Windows 95 starts the appropriate program, which in this case is Notepad, and opens the document so you can edit it.

To open the Phone Log:

1. Click the **Phone Log** icon, then press the **Enter** key. Windows 95 starts Notepad. See Figure 4-7.

Figure 4-7 ◀
Phone Log
document
opens in
Notepad

📋 **Phone Log - Notepad**   _ □ ✕

File   Edit   Search   Help

Creating a LOG File

Notepad automatically inserts the date when you open a document only if the document begins with .LOG, in uppercase letters. Your next step is to set up a document with .LOG at the beginning and enter some initial information. Then you will save the document and close it.

To set up the Phone Log document:

1. Type **.LOG**. *You must use uppercase letters.*

2. Press the **Enter** key to move to the next line.

3. Type **Phone Log for Beth Yuan**, then press the **Enter** key.

4. Click the **Close** button ☒ to close Notepad.

5. Click **Yes** to save the changes.

Now you should test the Phone Log document to see if an automatic date-time stamp appears when you open it.

To test the .LOG feature:

1. Open the **Phone Log** document.

TROUBLE? To open the Phone Log document, click it and press Enter or double-click it.

2. Make sure your document contains a date and time stamp. See Figure 4-8.

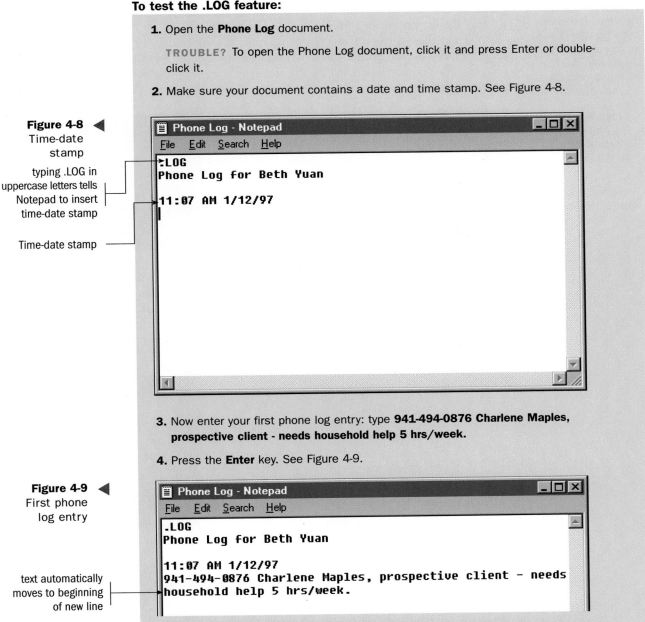

Figure 4-8 ◀
Time-date
stamp

typing .LOG in
uppercase letters tells
Notepad to insert
time-date stamp

Time-date stamp

3. Now enter your first phone log entry: type **941-494-0876 Charlene Maples, prospective client - needs household help 5 hrs/week.**

4. Press the **Enter** key. See Figure 4-9.

Figure 4-9 ◀
First phone
log entry

text automatically
moves to beginning
of new line

TROUBLE? If your text doesn't automatically move to a new line when it reaches the window border, as shown in Figure 4-9, click Edit, then click Word Wrap.

5. Click the **Close** button to close Notepad.

6. Click **Yes** to save the changes.

Creating Shortcuts to Objects

Beth uses her floppy drive regularly and would like an easier way to access it. It sounds like what she needs is a shortcut icon on the desktop to her floppy drive. A **shortcut icon** provides easy access to the objects on your computer you use most often. You can create shortcut icons for drives, documents, files, programs, or other computer resources such as a printer. These "shortcuts" reduce the number of mouse clicks needed to work with files, start programs, and print.

To create a shortcut, you use Windows Explorer to find the icon for the document, program, or resource for which you want a shortcut. Then you use the right mouse button to drag the icon onto the desktop.

As with other icons on the desktop, to activate a shortcut, you simply click it and press the Enter key or you double-click it. The shortcut locates and then opens the document, program, or resource specified by the shortcut icon. Shortcut icons are identified by the arrow in their lower-left corner, as shown in Figure 4-10.

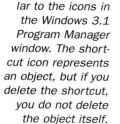

3.1 NOTE

Shortcuts are similar to the icons in the Windows 3.1 Program Manager window. The shortcut icon represents an object, but if you delete the shortcut, you do not delete the object itself.

Figure 4-10 ◄
Comparing shortcut icon to document icon

shortcut icon has small arrow in lower left corner

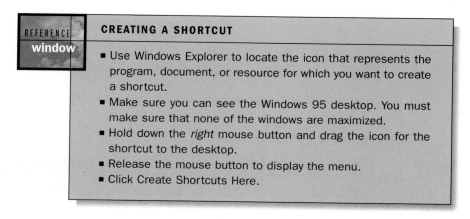

The shortcut icon on the left in Figure 4-10 is a shortcut to a document, whereas the document icon on the right is the *document itself*. You will learn more about this important distinction when you actually create a shortcut icon to a document later on.

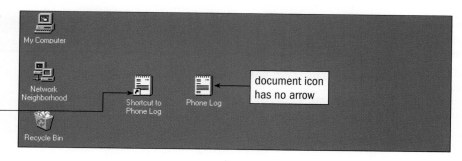

REFERENCE
window

CREATING A SHORTCUT

- Use Windows Explorer to locate the icon that represents the program, document, or resource for which you want to create a shortcut.
- Make sure you can see the Windows 95 desktop. You must make sure that none of the windows are maximized.
- Hold down the *right* mouse button and drag the icon for the shortcut to the desktop.
- Release the mouse button to display the menu.
- Click Create Shortcuts Here.

Creating a Shortcut to a Drive

Now you will create a shortcut to your floppy drive. Once this shortcut is on the desktop, you can open it to view the contents of your Student Disk, or you can move or copy documents to it without having to start Windows Explorer.

To create a shortcut to your floppy drive:

1. Start the Windows Explorer program.

    TROUBLE? To start Windows Explorer, click the Start button, point to Programs, then click Windows Explorer.

2. Make sure the Exploring window is open, but not maximized.

    TROUBLE? If the Exploring window is maximized, click 🗗 .

3. Place your Student Disk in drive A.

    TROUBLE? If your 3½-inch disk drive is B, place your Student Disk in that drive instead, and for the rest of the tutorial substitute drive B wherever you see drive A.

4. Locate the device icon 🖫 for 3½ Floppy (A:) in the Folders list on the left side of the Exploring window.

5. Hold down the *right* mouse button while you drag the device icon 🖫 for 3½ Floppy (A:) into an empty area of the desktop. The pointer looks like 🖫.

6. Release the mouse button. Notice the menu that appears, as shown in Figure 4-11.

Figure 4-11 ◄
Creating a
shortcut to
drive A

drag icon to an empty
area of the desktop
using the right
mouse button

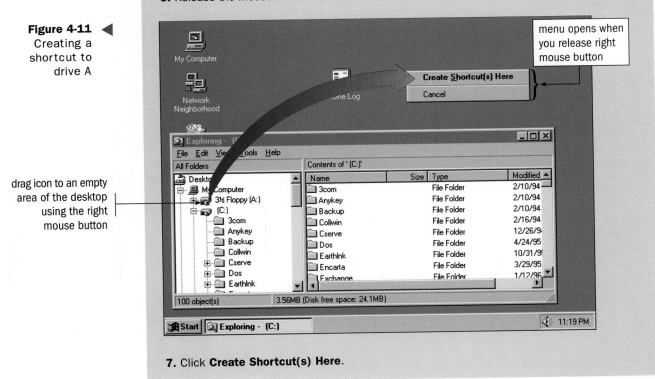

7. Click **Create Shortcut(s) Here**.

8. Click the **Close** button to close Windows Explorer. A shortcut labeled "Shortcut to 3½ Floppy (A:)" now appears on the desktop. See Figure 4-12.

Figure 4-12 ◄
Shortcut to
drive A

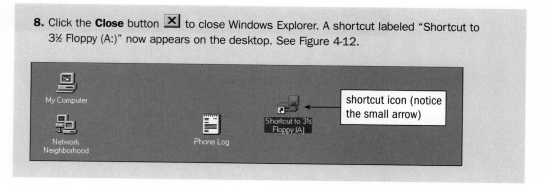

Now you can test the shortcut to see if it gives you immediate access to your Student Disk.

To test the 3½ Floppy (A:) shortcut:

1. Open **3½ Floppy (A:)** using the shortcut icon. A window showing the contents of your 3½ Floppy (A:) drive opens.

2. Click the **Close** button to close the 3½ Floppy (A:) window.

Using a Shortcut Icon

Beth often works out of her home office and needs to be able to take the phone log with her. You tell her the shortcut makes this easy. All she has to do is move the phone log from the desktop to a floppy disk using the shortcut.

You move a document from your desktop to your Student Disk by dragging it to the shortcut.

3.1 NOTE

Although Windows 3.1 allows dragging in a few isolated circumstances, such as moving a file from one open window to another, Windows 95 allows dragging in many more situations as you'll see in this tutorial.

To move the document from the desktop to a floppy disk:

1. Hold down the *right* mouse button and drag the **Phone Log** icon on the desktop to the 3½ Floppy (A:) shortcut you just created. When you release the right mouse button, a menu opens, as shown in Figure 4-13.

TROUBLE? If the Shortcut to 3½ Floppy (A:) icon is not highlighted, the Phone Log document will not move to drive A. Be sure the Shortcut to 3½ Floppy (A:) icon is highlighted, as shown in Figure 4-13, before you proceed to Step 2.

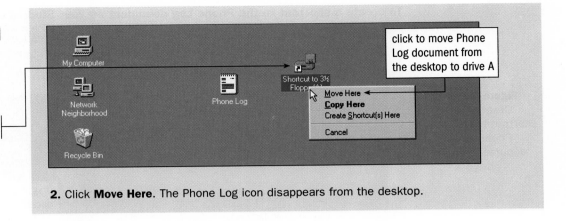

Figure 4-13 ◀
Moving the
Phone Log
document to
drive A

shortcut icon for drive
A is highlighted

click to move Phone
Log document from
the desktop to drive A

2. Click **Move Here**. The Phone Log icon disappears from the desktop.

When you moved the document icon to the drive A shortcut, the file itself was moved to drive A and off your desktop. You must access the Phone Log by opening drive A. You could open drive A from My Computer or Windows Explorer, but it is handier to use the drive A shortcut. Try using the shortcut method as you add an entry for another phone call.

To open the Phone Log document from the new 3½ Floppy (A:) window and add a new entry:

1. Open **3½ Floppy (A:)** using the shortcut icon to verify that the Phone Log document is on your Student Disk.

   TROUBLE? If you don't see the Phone Log document on your Student Disk, click the Undo Move button [icon] (or click Edit, then click Undo Move if the toolbar isn't displayed), then repeat the previous set of steps for moving a document to a floppy disk.

2. Open the **Phone Log** document from the 3½ Floppy (A:) window. Windows 95 starts Notepad.

3. Click the last line of the phone log so you can type a new entry.

4. Type **555-885-0876 Frank Meyers, next week's home care schedule.**

5. Click the **Close** button [X] to close Notepad.

6. Click **Yes** to save the changes.

Creating a Shortcut to a Document

The Phone Log document is now on a floppy disk, as Beth requested, but it no longer has an icon on the desktop. If you want to access the Phone Log document directly from the desktop, you can create a shortcut that automatically starts Notepad and opens the Phone Log from your Student Disk.

To create a shortcut to the Phone Log document on your Student Disk:

1. Hold down the *right* mouse button while you drag the Phone Log icon from the 3½ Floppy (A:) window onto the desktop, as shown in Figure 4-14, then release the mouse button.

Figure 4-14 ◄
Creating a
shortcut to the
Phone Log
document on
drive A

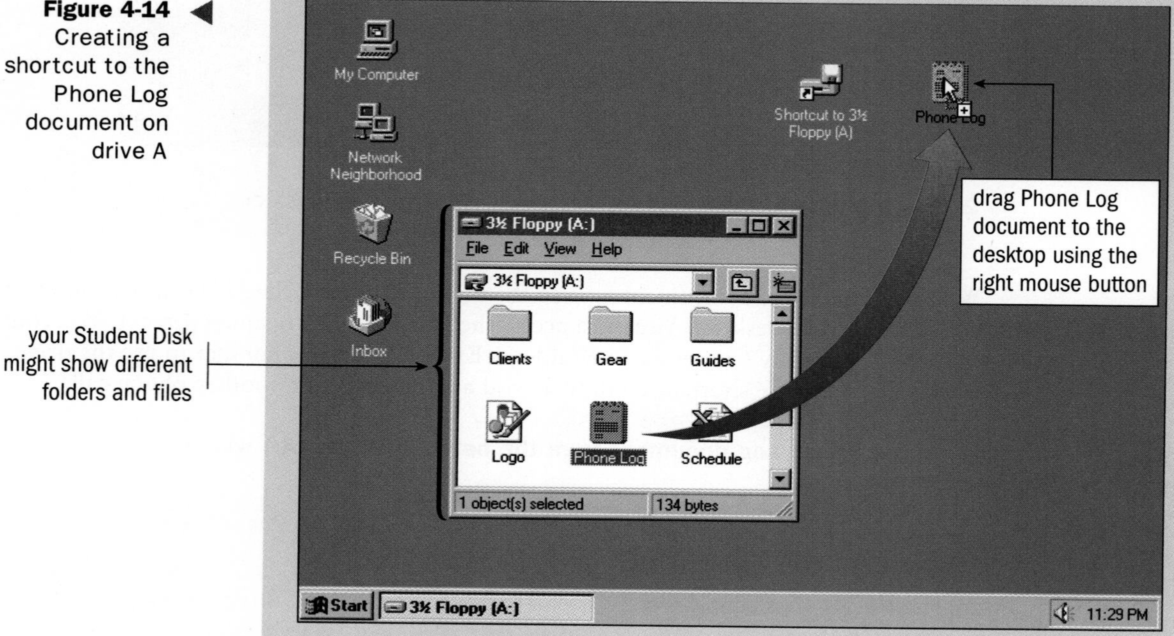

your Student Disk
might show different
folders and files

drag Phone Log
document to the
desktop using the
right mouse button

2. Click **Create Shortcut(s) Here**.

3. Click the **Close** button ⊠ to close the 3½ Floppy (A:) window. An icon labeled "Shortcut to Phone Log" now appears on the desktop.

You might wonder if dragging with the left mouse button creates a shortcut icon in the same way as dragging with the right mouse button. The answer is no. If you drag an icon onto the desktop using the left mouse button, you create a *copy* of the document on the desktop, not a *shortcut* to the document. This distinction is important to remember so that you don't find yourself working with a copy when you want to be working with the original. Now you can test the shortcut to see if it automatically opens the Phone Log.

To test the Phone Log shortcut:

1. Open the **Shortcut to Phone Log**. Windows 95 starts the Notepad program, then opens the Phone Log document.

2. Type: **313-892-7766 Trinity River Accounting** at the end of the list of calls.

3. Click the **Close** button ⊠ to close Notepad.

4. Click **Yes** to save the changes.

The shortcut icon you just created is different from the Phone Log icon you created at the beginning of this tutorial. That icon was not a shortcut icon. It was a document icon representing a document that was actually located right on the desktop. A shortcut icon, on the other hand, can represent a document located anywhere. The shortcut icon currently on your desktop represents a document located on your Student Disk. You can tell the difference between an actual document icon and a shortcut icon by looking for a small arrow in the corner of the icon. If there is no arrow, that icon represents the document. Glance back at Figure 4-10 to see this important difference.

If you delete a document icon, you also delete the document. If you delete a shortcut icon (with the arrow) you don't delete the document itself, you are just deleting the shortcut.

Creating a Shortcut to a Printer

You now have a very efficient way to open the Phone Log and to access your floppy drive. You're sure that Beth will be pleased when you tell her. But first you decide to add a printer shortcut to your growing collection of desktop icons so employees can easily print their phone logs and other documents.

You create a printer shortcut in much the same way as you created a shortcut for the floppy drive. First, you locate the printer icon in Windows Explorer. Then you use the right mouse button to drag the icon onto the desktop.

To create a Printer Shortcut:

1. Open Windows Explorer.

   TROUBLE? To open Windows Explorer, click the Start button, click Programs, then click Windows Explorer.

2. If the Exploring window is maximized, click the **Restore** button 🗗 so you can see part of the desktop.

3. Locate and then click the **Printers** folder. It is usually located at the bottom of the Folders list. See Figure 4-15.

Figure 4-15 ◀
Printers folder
in Windows
Explorer

Printers is highlighted ──────

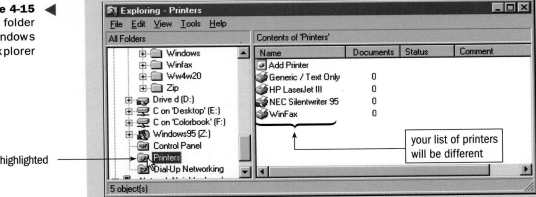

4. Position the pointer over the icon of the printer for which you want to create a shortcut.

   TROUBLE? If more than one printer is listed and you do not know which printer you usually use, ask your instructor or technical support person.

5. Hold down the *right* mouse button while you drag the printer icon to the desktop.

6. Release the right mouse button to drop the printer icon on the desktop.

7. Click **Create Shortcut(s) Here** on the menu. The printer shortcut appears. See Figure 4-16.

Figure 4-16 ◄
Creating a
shortcut to
a printer

drag printer to
desktop with the right
mouse button

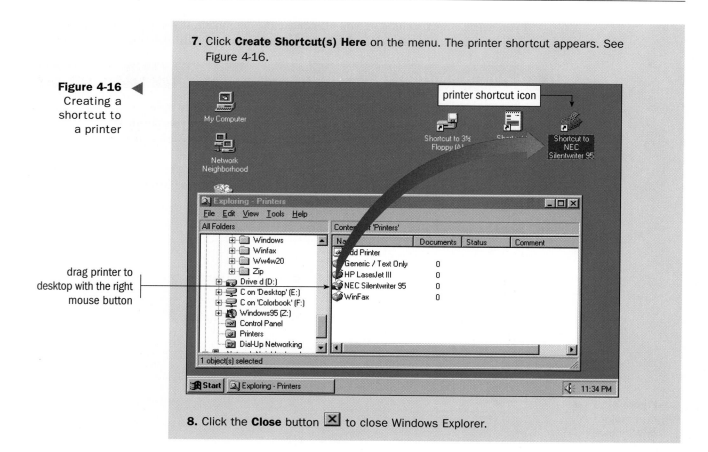

8. Click the **Close** button ⊠ to close Windows Explorer.

Once a printer icon is placed on the desktop, you can print a document by dragging its icon to the printer icon. Think of the steps you save by printing this way: you don't have to open any programs or search through menus to locate and open the document or the Print dialog box.

To print the Phone Log document using the printer shortcut:

1. Drag the **Phone Log** shortcut icon using the *left* mouse button to the Printers shortcut icon. See Figure 4-17.

Figure 4-17 ◄
Printing a
document
using shortcuts

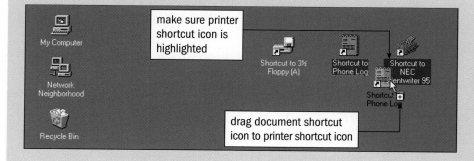

2. When you release the mouse button, watch as Windows 95 starts the Notepad program, opens the Phone Log, prints Phone Log, then closes Notepad. Because your document has an automatic time-date stamp, Windows 95 asks if you want to save the document before closing it. You don't need to save it because you don't have any phone entries to log.

3. Click **No**. Windows 95 closes Notepad without saving the time-date stamp.

Identifying Icons on the Desktop

Your desktop now has three new shortcut icons. Although the names of the shortcut icons help you identify what they are, the icons themselves help you identify the shortcut type. Figure 4-18 shows typical icons you might see on a desktop and the objects they represent.

Figure 4-18
Types of short-cut icons you might see on the desktop

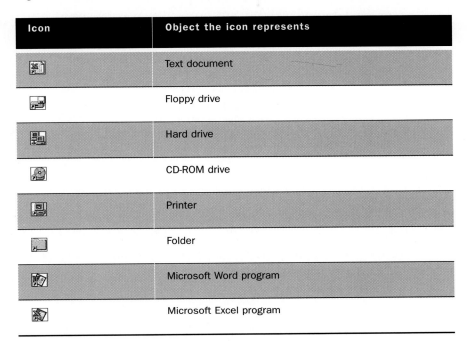

Icon	Object the icon represents
	Text document
	Floppy drive
	Hard drive
	CD-ROM drive
	Printer
	Folder
	Microsoft Word program
	Microsoft Excel program

   When you are opening a document represented by a desktop icon you can usually identify which program Windows 95 will start by looking at the icon representing the document.

Deleting Shortcut Icons

If you are working on your own computer you can leave the printer and drive icons in place if you think you'll find them useful. Otherwise, you should delete all the shortcuts you created so the desktop is clean for the next user. You can delete them one at a time by clicking a shortcut and then pressing the Delete key.

To delete your shortcuts:

   1. Click the printer shortcut icon with the *left* mouse button so that it is highlighted.

   2. Press the **Delete** key, then click **Yes** to delete the printer icon.

   3. Repeat Steps 1 and 2 with the floppy drive shortcut icon.

   4. Repeat Steps 1 and 2 with the phone log shortcut icon.

Your desktop is restored to its original appearance.

Quick Check

1. True or false? In a document-centric desktop, the quickest way to open a document is by locating the program that created the document, starting the program, and then using the Open command to locate and open the document.

2. True or false? You can create a document with an automatic time-date stamp in Notepad by typing "log" at the beginning of the document.

3. Name two ways to open a document on the desktop.

4. What happens if you delete a document icon that does not have an arrow on it?

5. What happens if you delete a shortcut icon?

6. What happens if you try to create a shortcut icon by dragging with the left mouse button instead of the right?

SESSION

4.2

In this session you'll change the appearance of your desktop by working with the desktop's property sheets. You'll experiment with patterns and wallpaper, enable a screen saver, try different colors to see how they look, and modify desktop settings to explore your monitor's capabilities.

Viewing Desktop Properties

In Windows 95, you can think of all the parts of your computer—the operating system, the programs, and the documents—as individual objects. For example, the desktop is an object, the taskbar is an object, a drive is an object, a program is an object, and a document is an object. Each object has **properties**, or characteristics, that you can examine and sometimes change. The desktop itself has many properties, including its color, its size, and the font it uses. Most objects in Windows 95 have property sheets associated with them. A **property sheet** is a dialog box that you open to work with an object's properties. To open an object's property sheet, you right-click the object and then click Properties on the menu.

3.1 NOTE

Property sheets are new with Windows 95. They offer easier, more intuitive, and more consistent access to object properties than Windows 3.1.

VIEWING AND CHANGING OBJECT PROPERTIES

- Right-click the object whose properties you want to view.
- Click Properties on the menu that opens.
- Click the tab for the property sheet you want to view.
- Change the appropriate settings.
- Click the Apply button to apply the changes and leave the property sheet open, or click the OK button to apply the changes and close the property sheet.

To view desktop properties:

1. Right-click an empty area of the desktop to open the menu. See Figure 4-19.

Figure 4-19 ◀
Desktop menu

right-click to view
desktop properties

menu opens when
you right-click empty
area of the desktop

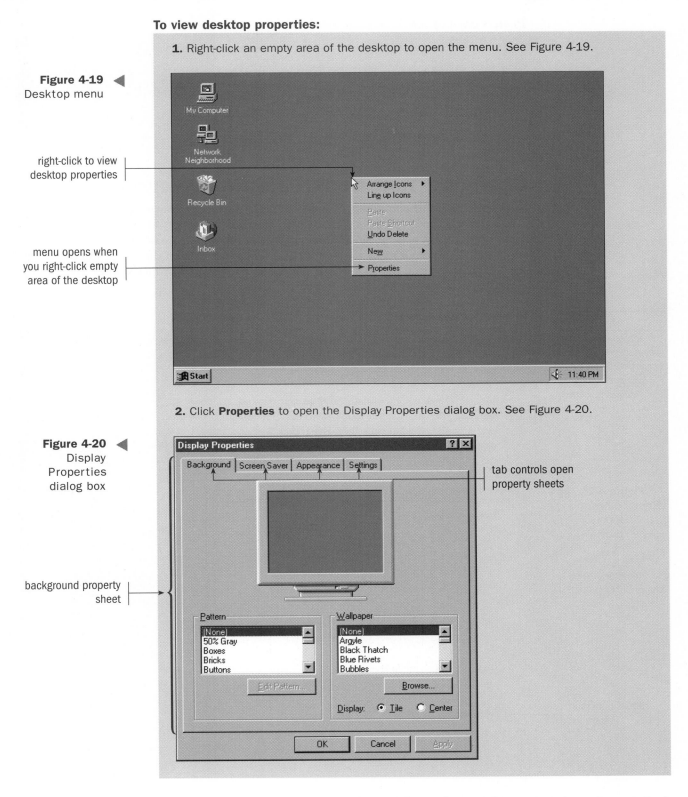

2. Click **Properties** to open the Display Properties dialog box. See Figure 4-20.

Figure 4-20 ◀
Display
Properties
dialog box

tab controls open
property sheets

background property
sheet

The Display Properties dialog box has four tab controls running along the top. Each tab corresponds to a property sheet. Some objects require only one property sheet, but the desktop has so many properties associated with it that there are four tabs. The Background tab appears first, displaying list boxes for the desktop background's pattern and wallpaper. To view a different property sheet, you click its tab.

To view each of the desktop property sheets:

1. Click the **Screen Saver** tab to view options for enabling a screen saver.

2. Click the **Appearance** tab to view options that affect the desktop's appearance.

3. Click the **Settings** tab to view options for the color palette, desktop fonts, and monitor resolution.

4. Click the **Background** tab to return to the first property sheet.

Changing Your Desktop's Background

Beth wants the staff computers in the Companions offices to have a corporate look. You can change the desktop background, which by default is a light forest green with no pattern. Alternatively, you can select a pattern or a graphic, called **wallpaper**, as a background design for your screen using the Pattern and Wallpaper lists on the Background property sheet. The image of a monitor at the top of the Background property sheet lets you preview the pattern or wallpaper you choose.

3.1 NOTE

Windows 95 can use any patterns installed previously by Windows 3.1, and also adds some new ones.

To select a pattern:

1. Click the **Bricks** pattern in the Pattern list. The monitor preview changes to show the Bricks pattern. See Figure 4-21.

   TROUBLE? If the Bricks pattern isn't available, choose a different one.

   TROUBLE? If you have installed Microsoft Plus! for Windows 95, you might have the Desktop Themes feature. You need to turn this feature off before you can work with patterns and backgrounds. Click Start, click Settings, then click Control Panel. Locate and open Desktop Themes, click the Theme list arrow, then click Windows Default. Close the Desktop Themes dialog box and the Control Panel, and repeat Step 1.

Figure 4-21 ◄
Bricks pattern
in monitor
preview

monitor preview
shows Bricks pattern

bricks pattern in
Pattern list

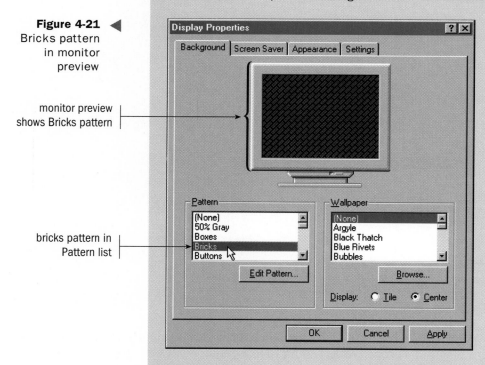

2. Scroll toward the bottom of the Pattern list, then click **Stone**. The monitor preview now shows the Stone pattern.

3. Click the **Apply** button to see how this pattern appears on the entire desktop. See Figure 4-22.

Figure 4-22 ◀
Stone pattern
applied to
desktop

monitor preview
shows Stone pattern

Stone pattern in
Pattern list

Stone pattern
on desktop

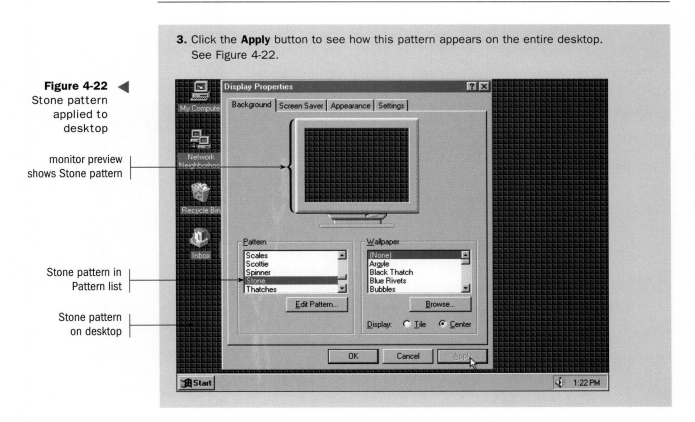

This pattern is not really what Beth wants. You decide to experiment with the Windows 95 wallpapers. Perhaps you can find one that matches Companions' corporate look.

To select a wallpaper:

1. Scroll to the top of the Pattern list, then click **(None)** to deselect the pattern.

2. Click **Bubbles** in the Wallpaper list. The monitor preview displays bubbles.

TROUBLE? If the Bubbles wallpaper isn't available, choose a different one.

3. Click the **Center** radio button to display one copy of the wallpaper image centered on the screen.

4. Click the **Tile** radio button to display multiple copies of the wallpaper image repeated across the entire screen.

5. Click the **OK** button. The resulting wallpaper, shown in Figure 4-23, is a little overwhelming. You know Beth wouldn't want this look, so you return to the Background property sheet to make a different selection.

Figure 4-23 ◄
Bubbles
wallpaper
applied to
desktop

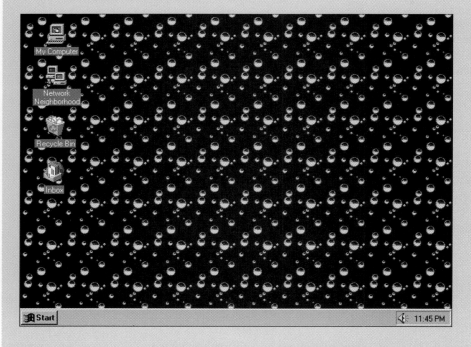

6. Right-click an empty area of the desktop, then click **Properties**.

7. Experiment with the wallpapers available on your computer by clicking them in the Wallpaper list and viewing them in the monitor preview.

8. Click **(None)** when you have exhausted the list, then click the **Apply** button.

None of the wallpapers that come with Windows 95 would suit Beth's corporate image, so you ask her if she would like to use the bitmap image of her company logo. She is enthusiastic; it would be great if clients who come to the offices could see the company logo on office computers.

REFERENCE window	**USING A BITMAP IMAGE AS CUSTOM WALLPAPER**

- Right-click an empty area of the desktop, then click Properties.
- Click the Background tab.
- Click the Browse button.
- Locate the folder containing the bitmap image you want to use as wallpaper, then click the bitmap image.
- Click the OK button.
- Click the Center radio button to center the image on the screen or the Tile radio button to display duplicate images.
- Click the OK button.

To use a bitmap image as custom wallpaper:

1. Place your Student Disk in **drive A**, then click the **Browse** button on the Background property sheet.

2. Click the **Drives** list arrow, click drive A, click the file **Logo.bmp**, then click the **OK** button. See Figure 4-24.

   TROUBLE? If your Student Disk does not contain the Logo file, use Quick Format to erase your Student Disk. Then click the Start button, point to Programs, point to CTI Windows 95 Applications, point to Windows 95 New Perspectives Introductory, then click Make Student Disk.

Figure 4-24 ◀
Locating the
bitmap image

Logo file ——

3. Click the **Center** radio button to center the image on the screen, then click the **OK** button to close the Display Properties dialog box. See Figure 4-25.

Figure 4-25 ◀
Companions
logo applied as
wallpaper

Changing Your Desktop's Appearance

Beth looks over your shoulder and comments that the red of the logo doesn't go very well with the green of the screen background, and she asks if you can try other background colors. The Appearance property sheet gives you control over the color not only of the desktop background but also of all the items on the screen: icons, title bars, borders, menus, scroll bars, and so on.

To view the Appearance property sheet:

1. Right-click an empty area of the desktop, then click **Properties**.

2. Click the **Appearance** tab. The Appearance property sheet is shown in Figure 4-26.

Figure 4-26 ◀
Appearance
property sheet

Scheme list box
displays current
scheme

any changes to
appearance you
make affect item
shown here

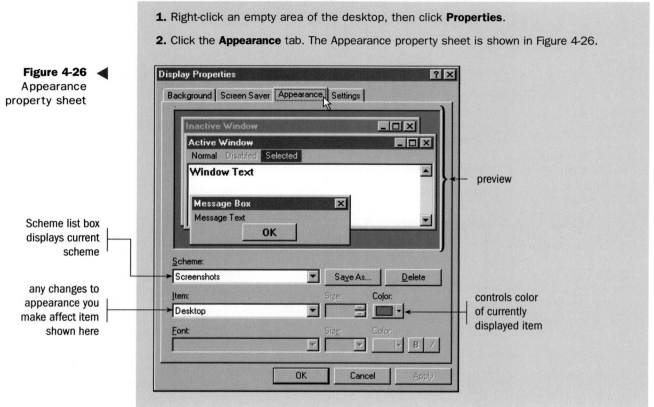

preview

controls color
of currently
displayed item

The Appearance property sheet includes several list boxes from which you choose options to change the desktop's appearance. Notice the Scheme list box. A **scheme** is a desktop design. Windows 95 includes a collection of design schemes. You can create your own by working with the Appearance property sheet until you arrive at a look you like, then using the Save As button. The default scheme is Windows Standard. However, if your computer is in a lab, your lab manager might have designed and selected a different scheme. Before you experiment with the appearance of your desktop, you should write down the current scheme so you can restore it later.

The preview in the Appearance property sheet displays many of the elements you are likely to see when working with Windows 95. You can click an item in the preview to change its color, and sometimes its font or size. You want to change the desktop itself to red. The Item list box currently displays "Desktop," so any changes you make in the Color list affect the desktop.

To change the color of your desktop to red:

1. Write down the name of the current scheme, which is displayed in the Scheme list box.

   TROUBLE? If your Scheme list box is empty, your lab manager might have changed scheme settings without saving the scheme. You should check with your lab manager before making any changes to the Appearance property sheet. If you get permission to change the scheme, make sure you record the original colors so you can restore them when you are finished.

2. Make sure the Item list box displays "Desktop."

   TROUBLE? If the Item list box does not display "Desktop," click the Item list arrow, scroll until you see "Desktop," then click Desktop.

3. Click the **Color** list arrow ▾, then click **red**, the first box in the second row. See Figure 4-27.

Figure 4-27 ◀
Changing the color of the desktop

Desktop is item you are changing

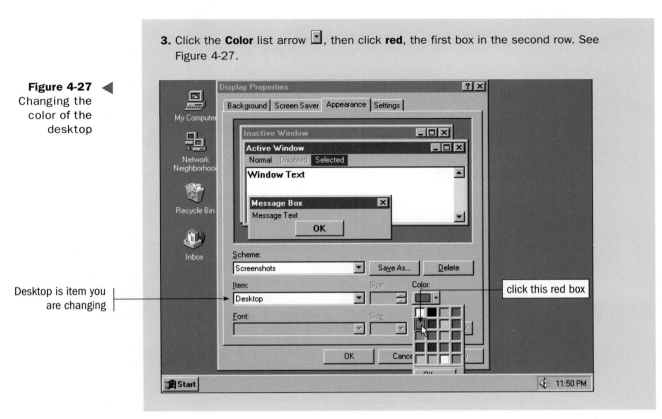

The desktop color in the preview changes to red. Notice that the Scheme list box is now empty because you are no longer using the current scheme. You notice that blue title bars looks strange in contrast to the red desktop. You decide to change the title bars to red as well. To change an element, you either click it in the preview or select it from the Item list.

To change the title bars to red:

1. Click the **Message Box title bar** in the preview. See Figure 4-28 for the location of this title bar. Note that the Item list box now displays "Active Title Bar."

2. Click the **Color** list arrow, then click **red**. See Figure 4-28.

Figure 4-28 ◀
Desktop with the new color applied

click this title bar to change color of active title bar

Scheme list box is empty

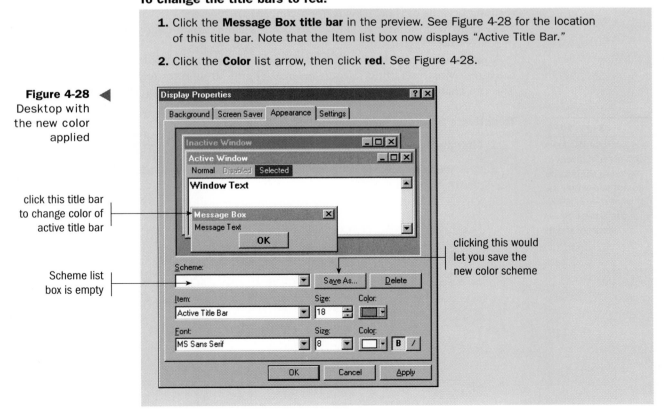

clicking this would let you save the new color scheme

3. Click the **OK** button to see how the desktop looks with a red background.

The next time you open a dialog box, you'll see a red title bar. Open the desktop property sheet to observe this. Then you should restore the desktop to its original settings. You can do this by simply selecting the scheme you wrote down earlier. You could save the colors that match Beth's logo as a scheme if you wanted to. You would click the Save As button, type a name for your scheme, and then click the OK button.

To restore the desktop colors and wallpaper to their original settings:

1. Right-click an empty area of the desktop, then click **Properties**.

2. Click the **Appearance** tab.

3. Click the **Scheme** list arrow, then locate and click the scheme you wrote down earlier. Most likely this is Windows Standard, which you will find at the bottom of the list.

TROUBLE? If your Scheme list box was blank when you began working with the Appearance property sheet, skip Step 3 and instead restore each setting you changed to its original color. Then proceed to Step 4.

4. Click the **Background** tab to open the Background property sheet.

5. Scroll to the top of the Wallpaper list, then click **(None)**.

6. Click the **Apply** button. The original desktop is restored.

Activating a Screen Saver

A **screen saver** blanks the screen or displays a moving design whenever the system sits idle for a specified period of time. In older monitors, a screen saver can help prevent 'burn-in' or the permanent etching of an image that is caused by the same image being displayed for long periods of time. This is not a concern with newer VGA monitors, but if you step away from your computer, the screen saver is handy for hiding your data from the eyes of passers-by.

You can determine how long you want the computer to sit idle before the screen saver activates. Most users find settings between 3 and 10 minutes to be the most convenient. You can change the setting by clicking the up or down arrow on the Wait box.

3.1 NOTE

You can use Windows 3.1 screen savers in Windows 95 but you do not see a preview of what they look like in the Screen Saver property sheet.

To activate a screen saver:

1. Click the **Screen Saver** tab.

2. Click the **Screen Saver** list arrow ▼ to display the list of available screen savers. See Figure 4-29.

Figure 4-29 ◄
Viewing
available
screen savers

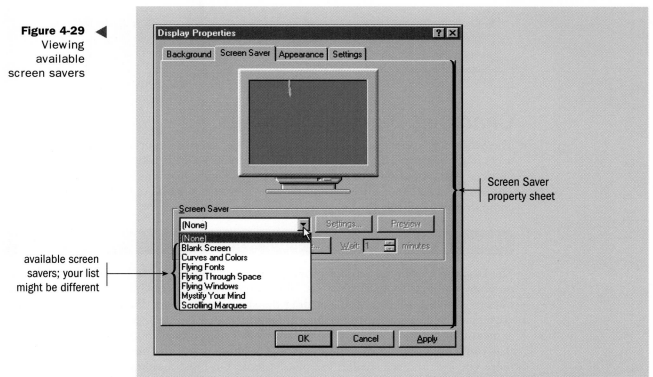

available screen
savers; your list
might be different

Screen Saver
property sheet

TROUBLE? If you don't see a list, your computer might have just one screen
saver installed. Don't worry.

3. Click any screen saver on the list to select it. Flying Windows is included on the
default installation, so click this selection if it is available.

4. Click the **Wait** up or down arrow to change the number in the Wait box to **5**. The
preview monitor shows how the screen saver will appear. See Figure 4-30.

Figure 4-30 ◄
Previewing a
screen saver

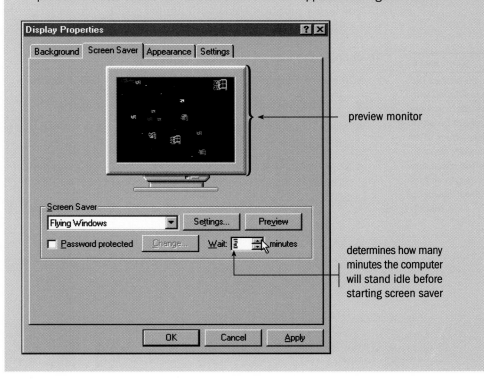

preview monitor

determines how many
minutes the computer
will stand idle before
starting screen saver

5. Click the **Cancel** button to cancel your screen saver changes. If you were working on your own computer and wanted to save the changes, you would click the Apply button to save the changes or the OK button to save the changes and close the Display Properties dialog box.

Changing Desktop Settings

The Settings property sheet gives you control over several important settings that casual users might never need to consider. However, if you want to take full advantage of your monitor type, you should be aware of the options you have on the Settings property sheet. The settings you can change depend on your monitor type and the **video card** inside your computer that controls the image you see on the screen.

Changing the Size of the Desktop Area

The Desktop area of the Settings property sheet lets you display less or more of the screen on your monitor. If you display less, objects will look bigger, while if you display more, objects will look smaller. You can drag the slider bar between these two extremes. You are actually increasing or decreasing the **resolution**, or sharpness, of the image. Resolution is measured by the number of individual dots, called **pixels**, short for picture elements, that run across and down your monitor. The more pixels the higher the resolution, the more you see, and the smaller the objects look. On most monitors in today's computer labs, the standard monitor resolution is 640 × 480: 640 pixels across and 480 down. This is the setting Beth's computers use.

The 640 × 480 resolution shows the least information, but uses the largest text and is preferred by most users with 14" monitors. The 800 × 600 resolution shows more information but uses smaller text. Many users with 15" monitors prefer the 800 × 600 resolution. The 1024 × 768 resolution shows the most information but uses the smallest text. Most users find the 1024 × 768 resolution too small for comfort unless they are using a 17" or larger monitor. Users with limited vision even on larger monitors might prefer the 640 × 480 setting because objects and text are bigger and easier to see.

3.1 NOTE

When you change the resolution with Windows 3.1 you have to reboot before it takes effect. With Windows 95, you can change the resolution on many monitors without having to reboot.

To change the size of the desktop area:

1. Right-click an empty area of the desktop, then click **Properties**.

2. Click the **Settings** tab to display the Settings properties.

3. Make a note of the original setting in the Desktop area so that you can restore it after experimenting with it.

4. To select the 640 × 480 resolution, drag the **Desktop area** slider to the left. The preview monitor shows the relative size of the 640 × 480 display. See Figure 4-31.

Figure 4-31 ◀
640×480
resolution

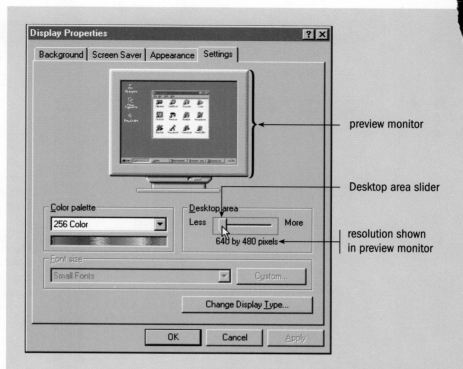

preview monitor

Desktop area slider

resolution shown
in preview monitor

5. To select the intermediate 800×600 resolution, drag the **Desktop area** slider to
the center or all the way to the right. The preview monitor shows the relative size
of the 800×600 display. See Figure 4-32.

Figure 4-32 ◀
800×600
resolution

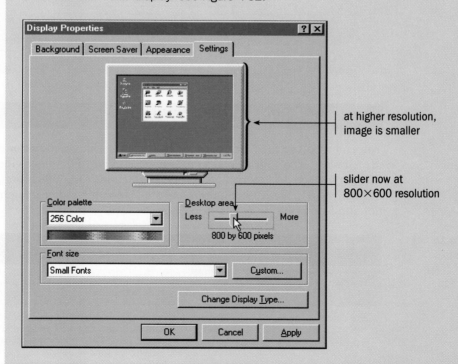

at higher resolution,
image is smaller

slider now at
800×600 resolution

6. To select the 1024×768 resolution, drag the **Desktop area** slider to the right.
The preview monitor shows the relative size of the 1024×768 display as shown
in Figure 4-33.

TROUBLE? If the 1024×768 resolution doesn't appear, your monitor might not support this setting. Skip Step 6. You also might have higher resolutions available. You can test them yourself by selecting them the same way you selected the resolutions in the preceding Steps.

Figure 4-33 ◀
1024×768
resolution

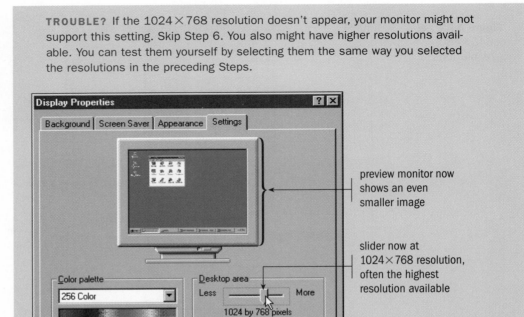

preview monitor now shows an even smaller image

slider now at 1024×768 resolution, often the highest resolution available

7. Return the slider to the original position. On most computers this is the 640×480 resolution.

Changing the Color Palette

You can also use the Settings property sheet to change the **color palette**, which specifies the number of colors available to your computer. For most video cards, the available palettes include 16 colors, 256 colors, High Color (32,000 colors), and True Color (16.7 million colors). Beth's computers have a 256-color palette. Figure 4-34 provides additional information on common palettes.

Figure 4-34 ◀
Color palettes

Palette	Description
16 colors	Very fast, requires the least video memory, sufficient for use with most programs but not adequate for most graphics.
256 colors	Relatively fast, requires a moderate amount of video memory, sufficient for most programs and adequate for the graphics in most games and educational programs. This is a good setting for general use.
High Color (32,000 colors)	Requires an accelerated video card and additional video memory. This setting is useful for sophisticated painting, drawing, and graphics manipulation tasks.
True Color (16.7 million colors)	Requires the most video memory and runs the slowest. This setting is useful for professional graphics tasks, but might not be available or might be too slow on many computer systems.

To view the color palette options:

1. Click the **Color palette** list arrow ▾ to display the list of color palettes. See Figure 4-35.

Figure 4-35 ◄
Available color palettes

available color palettes; your list might be different (band is hidden underneath)

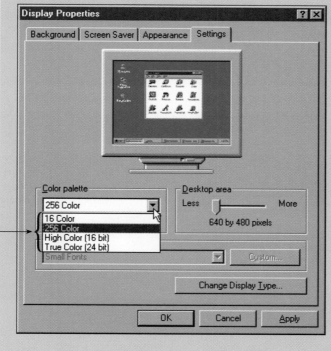

2. Click each option on the list and watch the color band below the Color palette list box change.

TROUBLE? If the band does not change when you select a different color palette, your monitor or video card doesn't support the selected color palette.

3. Click the **Color palette** list arrow again to close the list.

If you actually wanted to change the Color palette, you would have to reboot Windows 95. You should not change the Color palette setting in a computer lab.

Using Energy-saving Features

Some computer systems come with energy-saving features that power down components of your computer automatically when they've been idle for a specified time period. Computer components such as monitors that support energy-saving features are called **Energy Star compliant** and are often identified by a special Energy Star compliant sticker ⬟. Windows 95 includes two energy-saving features for Energy Star compliant monitors. You can find these features on the Screen Saver property sheet, if your monitor is Energy Star compliant. The first, called Low-power standby, switches your monitor to a mode that requires less power. The second feature, called Shut off monitor, shuts off your monitor after a specified period of idleness. When you tell Beth about these features, she is eager to implement them on the Companions computers, because they conserve both energy and money.

If you are in a computer lab, you can take a look at the property sheet to see if these features are available, but *do not* change them.

To view energy-saving features:

1. Click the **Screen Saver** tab. The energy-saving features appear at the bottom of the dialog box. See Figure 4-36.

Figure 4-36 ◄
Energy-saving
features

sticker that looks like this appears on Energy Star compliant components

switches your monitor to a mode requiring less power

energy-saving features might not appear on your computer if your monitor doesn't support them

shuts your monitor off

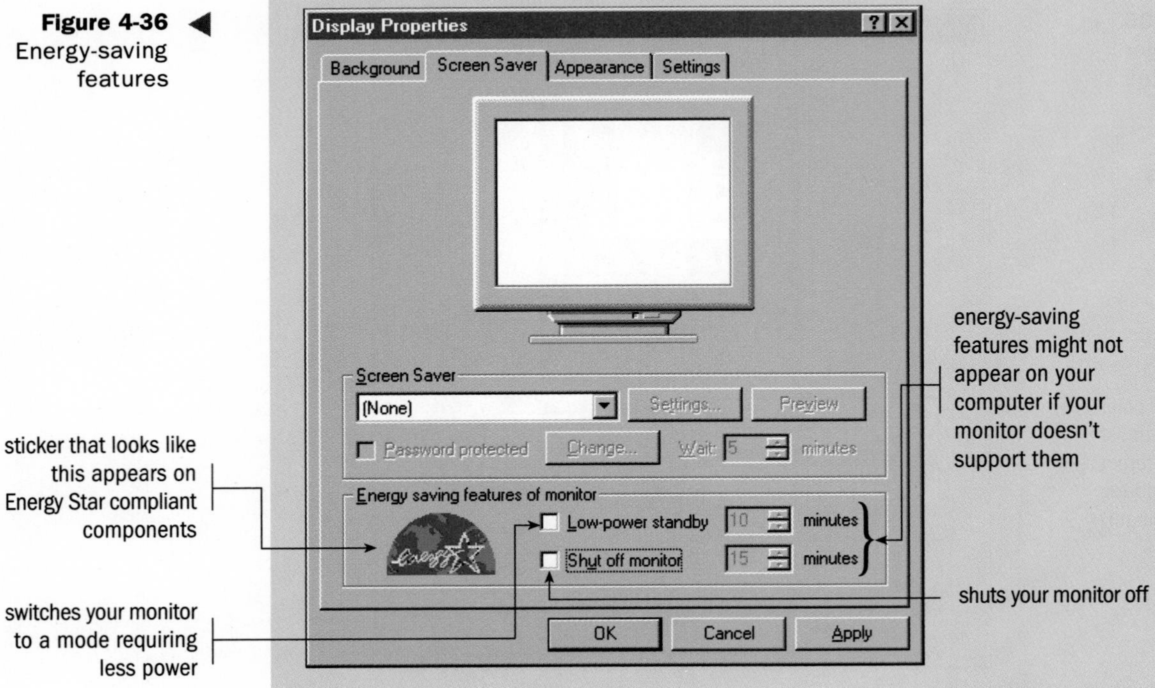

TROUBLE? If there is no Energy saving features area in your Screen Saver property sheet, your monitor might not be Energy Star compliant. If you think your monitor does support these features but the Energy saving features don't appear, click the Settings tab, and then click Change Display Type. Make sure the Monitor is Energy Star compliant check box is checked. Return to the Settings property sheet. If the area still doesn't appear, you might have the wrong monitor or adapter type selected. You can check this setting in the Change Display Type dialog box, but you should change this setting only if you are sure what monitor and adapter type you have.

2. If you are on your own computer and you want to enable this feature, click the **Low-power standby** check box to switch your monitor to standby after the period of time specified in the corresponding spin box.

3. If you are on your own computer and you want to enable this feature, click the **Shut off monitor** check box to turn off your monitor after the period of time specified in the corresponding spin box.

4. Click the **Cancel** button to close the Display Properties dialog box without making any further changes to your desktop.

If you have your own computer, you can combine screen-saver and energy-saving features. For example, you could specify five minute intervals for the three features: after five minutes your screen saver turns on, after 10 minutes your monitor goes into standby mode, and after 15 minutes your monitor shuts off.

Quick Check

1 True or false? Although a document is an object, and so is a drive, the desktop is not an object.

2 How do you open an object's property sheet?

3 Name three desktop properties you can change with the desktop property sheets.

4 If you have an older monitor and you want to protect it from harm caused by the same image being displayed for a long time, what can you do?

5 What does it mean to say a monitor's resolution is 640×480?

6 Users with limited vision might want to use which resolution: 640×480, 800×600, or 1024×768? Why?

7 What is the disadvantage of using a color palette with the most possible colors, like True Color, which can display 16.7 million colors on a monitor?

8 If you are shopping for a new monitor and want to make sure you can use the Windows 95 power-saving features on it, what sticker should you look for on the package?

SESSION

4.3

Windows 95 lets you further increase productivity by giving you control over your working environment. Customizing mouse settings can make some operations, especially graphics operations, easier. Depending on whether you are left- or right-handed, you might want to change other mouse settings. You might also want to take advantage of a variety of accessibility options, depending on your circumstances. In this session, you'll use the Control Panel to locate and adjust some of these settings.

Using the Control Panel

Windows 95 includes a **Control Panel**, available through the Start menu, that centralizes many of your computer's operations and customization features. You'll find the property sheets for many objects, including the desktop, on the Control Panel, as well as other tools that help you control your computer's settings. The Control Panel is so useful that you might want to place a shortcut to it on your desktop.

REFERENCE window

USING THE CONTROL PANEL TO CUSTOMIZE SETTINGS

- Click Start, point to Settings, then click Control Panel.
- Click the setting you want to work with, then press Enter.
- Change the settings in the dialog box that opens.
- Click OK.

To open the Control Panel:

1. Make sure you are at the Windows 95 desktop and no windows are open.

2. Click the **Start** button ![Start], point to **Settings**, then click **Control Panel**.

   TROUBLE? If a message appears indicating that the Control Panel is not available, you might be in a computer lab with limited customization access. Ask your instructor or lab manager for options.

3. Click **View**, then click **List** to display the icons as in Figure 4-37.

   TROUBLE? Because some tools are optional, your Control Panel might display different tools than the ones shown in Figure 4-37.

Figure 4-37 ◀
Control Panel

list of available tools;
yours might be
different

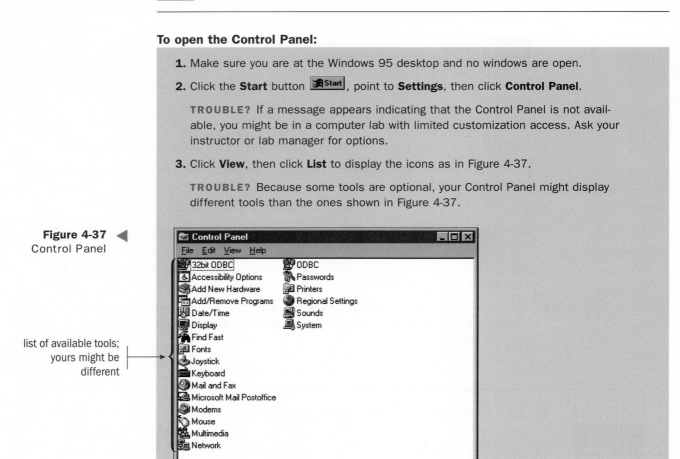

Customizing the Mouse

The Mouse Properties dialog box, available through the Control Panel, lets you customize the mouse settings. You can configure it for the right or left hand, you can adjust the double-click speed, you can turn on pointer trails to make it easier to locate the pointer, and you can adjust the pointer speed. Beth, and two of her employees, are left-handed, so one of the first things you want to do is experiment with the left-handed mouse settings.

Configuring the Mouse for the Right or Left Hand

You can configure the mouse for either right-handed or left-handed users. If you select the left-handed setting, the operations of the left and right mouse buttons are reversed. If you are instructed to click the *right* mouse button, you must click the *left* mouse button, and vice versa. *Check with your instructor or lab manager before you change this setting on a school lab computer, and make sure to change it back before you leave.*

To configure the mouse for right-handed or left-handed users:

1. Click the **Mouse** icon in the Control Panel, then press the **Enter** key to display the Mouse Properties dialog box. You can set the mouse for right-handed users or left-handed users by clicking the appropriate radio button. See Figure 4-38.

Figure 4-38 ◀
Buttons
property sheet

options that
determine left-
handed or right-
handed mouse
operations

descriptions of
mouse operations

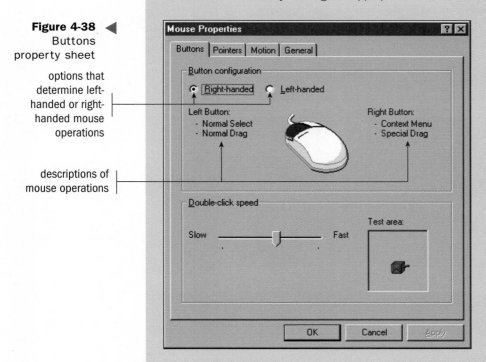

2. Click the **Right-handed** radio button if you are right-handed; click the **Left-handed** radio button if you are left-handed. Notice that as you change this setting the descriptions of mouse operations in the preview change.

3. If you are working on your own computer, click the **Apply** button to apply your changes, then test the new mouse setting by dragging the **Mouse Properties** dialog box with the appropriate mouse button.

4. Return this setting to its original state, then click the **Apply** button.

   TROUBLE? If clicking Apply doesn't seem to work, try using the other mouse button!

Adjusting Double-Click Speed

Double-clicking is equivalent to clicking an object and pressing Enter, or right-clicking an object and clicking Open. Many new users have difficulty double-clicking, which is why Microsoft designed Windows 95 to work without double-clicking. However, some users find double-clicking the quickest way to work. Beth wants you to experiment with slowing down the double-click speed.

To test the current double-click speed:

1. Position the pointer over the purple box in the Test area of the Mouse Properties dialog box, as shown in Figure 4-39.

Figure 4-39 ◀
Testing double-click speed

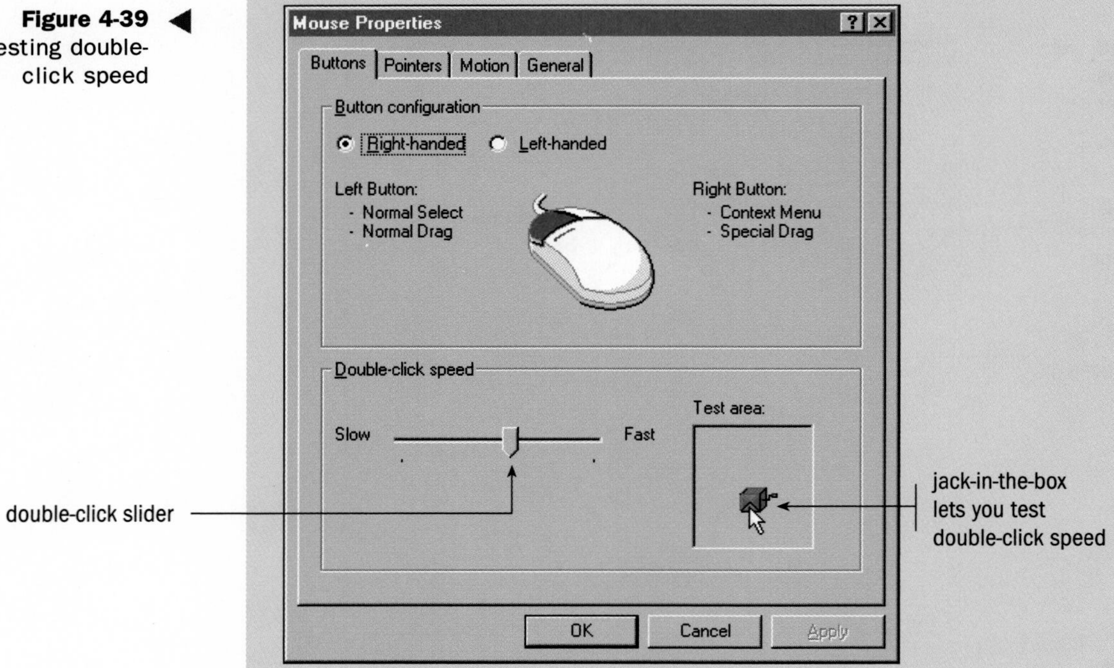

double-click slider

jack-in-the-box lets you test double-click speed

2. Place your hand on the mouse and quickly press and release the left mouse button twice.

TROUBLE? If you changed the mouse to left-handed operation, you will need to double-click by quickly pressing and releasing the *right* mouse button twice.

3. If you double-click successfully, the jack-in-the-box pops out of the box.

4. Double-click the **purple box** again to close it.

TROUBLE? Don't worry if you can't open the jack-in-the-box. In the next series of steps you'll learn how to adjust the double-click speed for your convenience.

If you have trouble double-clicking, you can slow down the double-click speed using the Double-click speed slider bar. *Check with your instructor or lab manager before you change this setting on a school lab computer, and make sure to change it back before you leave.*

To slow down the double-click speed:

1. Drag the **Double-click speed** slider toward Slow. This lets you take more time between the two clicks.

2. Double-click the **jack-in-the-box** to see if you can make it pop up.

3. If you still cannot successfully double-click, drag the **Double-click speed** slider even farther toward Slow, then repeat Step 2.

4. Once you can successfully double-click, try increasing or decreasing the double-click speed to find the most comfortable speed for you.

5. If you are using your own computer, click the **Apply** button to change the double-click speed to the new setting.

Using Pointer Trails

A **pointer trail** is a trail of pointers that appears on the screen in the wake of the pointer as you move it, like the wake of a boat. Locating the pointer is sometimes difficult, especially on some notebook computer displays. You might find the pointer trail helpful if you occasionally have trouble locating the pointer on your screen. For example, if Beth is on a business trip, she might enable the pointer trail while she uses her notebook computer in a dimly lit hotel room. Users with vision problems might also find this feature helpful. *Check with your instructor or lab manager before you change this setting on a school lab computer, and make sure to change it back before you leave.*

3.1 NOTE

Pointer trails are the same thing as Mouse Trails in Windows 3.1.

To turn on the pointer trail:

1. From the Mouse Properties dialog box, click the **Motion** tab to display the Motion property sheet. See Figure 4-40.

Figure 4-40 ◀
Motion
property sheet

click to show
pointer trails

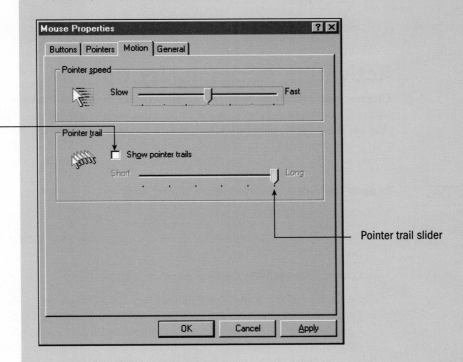

Pointer trail slider

2. Click the **Show pointer trails** check box.

3. Move the mouse. A trail of pointers follows the pointer when you move it.

4. To increase the length of the trail, drag the **Pointer trail slider** toward Long.

5. To decrease the length of the trail, drag the **Pointer trail slider** toward Short.

6. Click the **Apply** button if you want to leave pointer trails on, or, if you prefer to work without pointer trails, click the **Show pointer trails** check box again to remove the check mark.

Adjusting Pointer Speed

You can also adjust the pointer speed or the relative distance that the pointer moves on the screen when you move the mouse. *Check with your instructor or lab manager before you change this setting on a school lab computer, and make sure to change it back before you leave.*

To adjust the pointer speed:

1. Make sure the the Motion tab of the Mouse Properties dialog box is displayed.

2. To decrease the pointer speed, drag the **Pointer speed slider** toward Slow.

3. To increase the pointer speed, drag the **Pointer speed slider** toward Fast.

4. Adjust the pointer speed to the setting that is most comfortable for you, then click the **Apply** button.

5. Click the **OK** button to close the Mouse Properties dialog box.

Activating Accessibility Options

There is one other way you can customize the mouse in Windows 95: you can set the numeric keypad to take over some of the functions of the mouse. This option is not available on the Mouse property sheet. Instead, you need to open the Accessibility Options dialog box from the Control Panel. In this dialog box, Windows 95 includes many accessibility options that make computers easier to use for people with disabilities.

3.1 NOTE

Accessibility options are new with Windows 95.

To open the Accessibility Options dialog box:

1. Make sure the Control Panel is open.

   TROUBLE? If the Control Panel is not open, click the Start button, click Settings, then click Control Panel.

2. Click the **Accessibility Options** icon in the Control Panel.

   TROUBLE? If the Accessibility Options icon does not appear in the Control Panel, you might need to ask your lab manager to install Accessibility Options. If you are working on your own computer, you can install it yourself. Click the Add/Remove Programs icon in the Control Panel, click Windows Setup, then click Accessibility Options, click the OK button, then follow the instructions on the screen to install Accessibility Options from the original disks.

3. Press **Enter** to display the Accessibility Options dialog box. See Figure 4-41.

Figure 4-41 ◀
Accessibility
Options dialog
box

your available
property sheets might
be slightly different

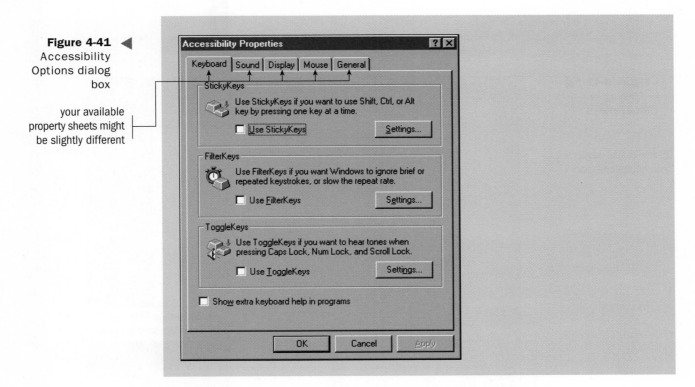

There are five property sheets available through the Accessibility Options dialog box: Keyboard, Sound, Display, Mouse, and General. Don't worry if you don't have all these tabs. In this session you explore some of the most helpful accessibility options. For example, if you have restricted movement, you can use the keyboard instead of the mouse and can simplify some key press sequences. If you have limited vision, you can select high-contrast mode to make it easier to see the objects and text on the screen.

Using Keys to Control the Pointer

All users occasionally have trouble using the mouse to precisely control the pointer when using programs such as Paint or other drawing or graphics programs. You can turn on MouseKeys to control the pointer with the numeric keypad as well as with the mouse. This is also a useful feature if you have a temporary or permanent hand injury.

To turn on MouseKeys:

1. Click the **Mouse** tab in the Accessibility Properties dialog box.

2. Click the **Use MouseKeys** check box to place a check mark in it.

3. Click the **Apply** button to activate MouseKeys. After a short time, the MouseKeys icon appears at the right end of the taskbar. See Figure 4-42.

Figure 4-42 ◀
Turning on
MouseKeys

click to control pointer
with numeric keypad

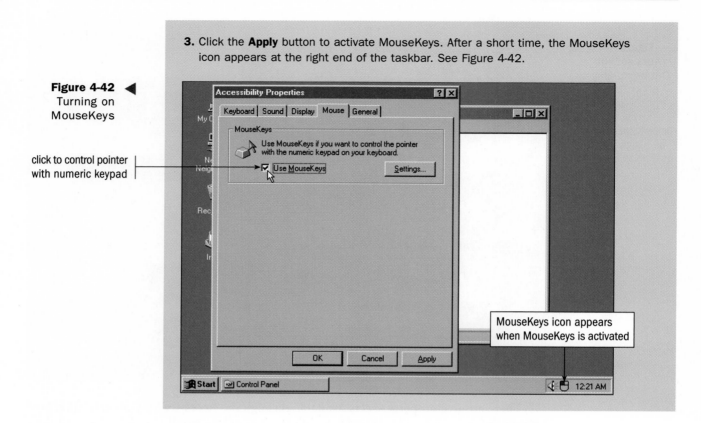

MouseKeys icon appears
when MouseKeys is activated

When the MouseKeys feature is active, you can control the pointer using either the mouse or the keys on the numeric keypad. Before you try working with MouseKeys, study Figure 4-43, which summarizes the mouse actions you can duplicate using keys on the numeric keypad.

Figure 4-43 ◀
MouseKeys
actions and
corresponding
keys

Mouse Action	Corresponding Numeric Keypad Key
Move pointer horizontally	Press 4 to move left, 6 to move right
Move pointer vertically	Press 8 to move up, 2 to move down
Move pointer diagonally	Press 7, 1, 9, and 3
Click	Press 5
Double-click	Press + (plus)
Right-click	Press – (minus), then press 5
Begin dragging after pointing to object	Press 0
End dragging	Del
Move a single pixel at a time	Press and hold Shift, then use directional keys

To practice using MouseKeys:

1. Use the numeric keypad to move the pointer over the **Start** button. The End key moves you to the lower left.

   TROUBLE? Most keyboards have two keypads: one with only arrows and one with numbers and arrows. Make sure you are using the keypad with numbers. If the pointer doesn't move when you press the number keys, press the NumLock key on the keyboard.

   TROUBLE? If you waited very long to start using MouseKeys, it's possible that Windows 95 is set to reset accessibility options after a specified amount of time. Return to the Mouse property sheet, and then reset MouseKeys by clicking Apply. Then click the General tab, and check if Automatic reset is enabled. If it is, click the check box to turn it off for now.

2. Press **5** once the pointer is over the Start button.

3. Hold down the **8** key to move the pointer to **Programs**, then press **5**.

4. Move the pointer to **Accessories**, then press **5**.

5. Move the pointer to **Paint**, then press **5** to start the Paint program.

6. Practice moving the pointer by pressing the **7 8 9, 4 6,** and **1 2 3** number keys on the numeric keypad.

7. Press the **0** key on the numeric keypad to start drawing. Press the number keys to move the pointer and draw precise vertical, horizontal, and diagonal lines. See Figure 4-44.

Figure 4-44 ◀
Drawing in Paint using MouseKeys

draw any shape you want

pressing number keys moves this pointer

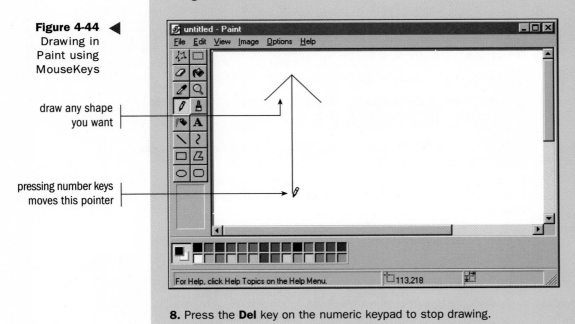

8. Press the **Del** key on the numeric keypad to stop drawing.

MouseKeys is especially useful for drawing precise diagonal lines in a graphics package like Paint, although, as you've probably discovered, it is slower. Now close Paint and deactivate MouseKeys.

To use MouseKeys to close the Paint window:

1. Use the keys on the numeric keypad to move the pointer over the **Close** button ☒ on the Paint window.

2. Press the **5** key to click ☒.

3. Use the keys on the numeric keypad to move the pointer over the **No** button on the Paint dialog box, then press the **5** key to close Paint.

4. Click the **Use MouseKeys** check box to turn this feature off.

Simplifying Key Operation with StickyKeys

StickyKeys is a feature that makes Windows 95 easier for users who have trouble holding down one key while pressing another key. Three keys typically used in conjunction with other keys are the Shift key, the Ctrl key, and the Alt key. These keys are also known as **modifier keys**—you hold them down while pressing another key to modify the action of the second key. Many actions that you perform with the mouse can also be performed with modifier keys. For example, instead of clicking the Start button to open the Start menu, you can use Ctrl+Esc. Keys combinations such as these are often called **keyboard shortcuts**. To more clearly show the effect of StickyKeys, you'll start by using a keyboard shortcut without StickyKeys enabled.

To test the normal behavior of a modifier key:

1. Click the **Control Panel** button on the taskbar to bring the Control Panel window to the foreground.

2. Notice the underlined character in each word on the menu bar. For example, notice the underlined F in File and the underlined V in View. You can use the underlined character with a modifier key to open the menu in a single step.

3. Press and hold the **Alt** key, then press **F** to display the File menu.

4. Press **Esc** to close the File menu.

5. Click the **Minimize** button ▬ to minimize the Control Panel window.

Now try enabling StickyKeys to see how it affects the way you use key combinations such as Alt+F.

To turn on StickyKeys:

1. Click the **Keyboard** tab in the Accessibility Properties dialog box to display the Keyboard properties.

2. Click the **Use StickyKeys** check box to place a check mark in it.

3. Click the **Apply** button to activate StickyKeys. After a few moments the StickyKeys icon appears in the bottom right corner of the taskbar. See Figure 4-45.

Figure 4-45
Activating
StickyKeys

click to control the
use of modifier keys

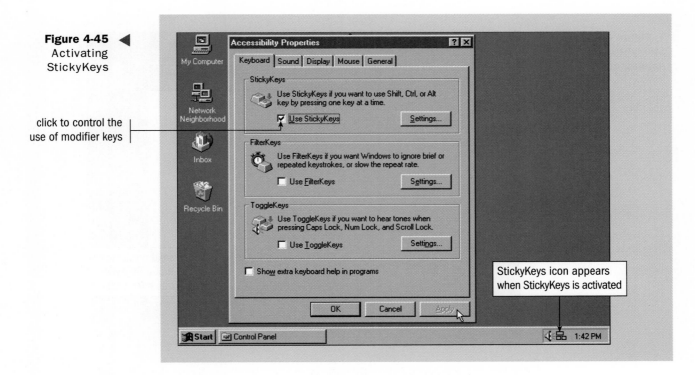

Once StickyKeys is enabled, you can press and release the modifier key and then press the action key to take the place of the keyboard shortcut. When you press the modifier key, the lower-right key in the StickyKeys icon is shaded.

To test the effect of StickyKeys:

1. Click the **Control Panel** button on the taskbar to bring the Control Panel window to the foreground.

2. Press and release the **Alt** key. A sound indicates that a StickyKey has been pressed and the bottom right box in the StickyKeys icon is filled in. See Figure 4-46. The sound and the icon indicate that the next key you press will be combined with the Alt StickyKey.

   TROUBLE? If you didn't hear a sound, sounds might not be enabled on your StickyKeys settings. You can enable sounds by clicking the Settings button in the Keyboard property sheet and selecting the sound settings you want.

Figure 4-46 ◀
StickyKey has
been pressed

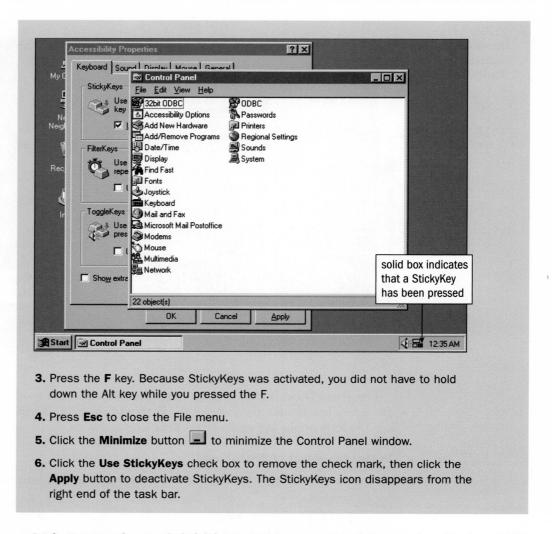

solid box indicates
that a StickyKey
has been pressed

3. Press the **F** key. Because StickyKeys was activated, you did not have to hold down the Alt key while you pressed the F.

4. Press **Esc** to close the File menu.

5. Click the **Minimize** button ▬ to minimize the Control Panel window.

6. Click the **Use StickyKeys** check box to remove the check mark, then click the **Apply** button to deactivate StickyKeys. The StickyKeys icon disappears from the right end of the task bar.

StickyKeys can be very helpful for users who want to use shortcut keys but have difficulty holding down one key while pressing another.

Enabling High Contrast

The Display property sheet lets you set the screen display to high contrast. **High contrast** uses large white letters on a black background and greatly increases the size of the title bar and window control buttons. In high-contrast mode, objects and text stand out more visibly. If you have limited vision, a dark office, or you're not wearing your glasses, high-contrast mode can make it much easier to see what's on your screen.

To turn on high contrast:

1. Click the **Display** tab to see the display properties.

2. Click the **Use High Contrast** check box to place a check mark in it.

3. Click the **Apply** button to activate the high-contrast settings. After a short time, the screen changes to the high-contrast display. See Figure 4-47.

Figure 4-47
Applying high
contrast

larger letters

color contrast is
more intense

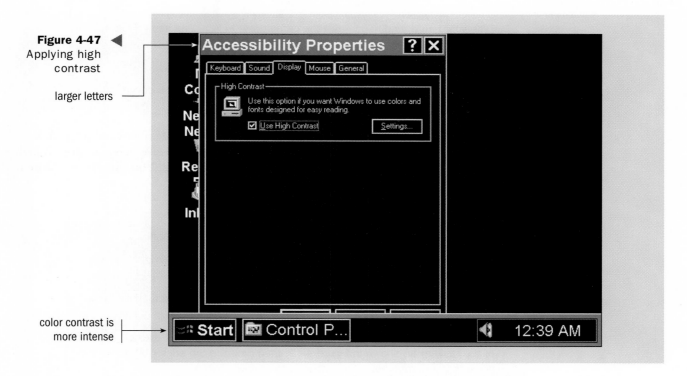

The high-contrast setting affects all programs, but it does not affect the contents of the document window in a program. Try opening WordPad to see how high contrast works in a program.

To run WordPad with high contrast active:

1. Click the **Start** button, point to **Programs**, then point to **Accessories**.

2. Click **WordPad** to start the WordPad program. WordPad appears as shown in Figure 4-48.

Figure 4-48
Opening a
program in high
contrast

default font in
WordPad will not
change when you
type something

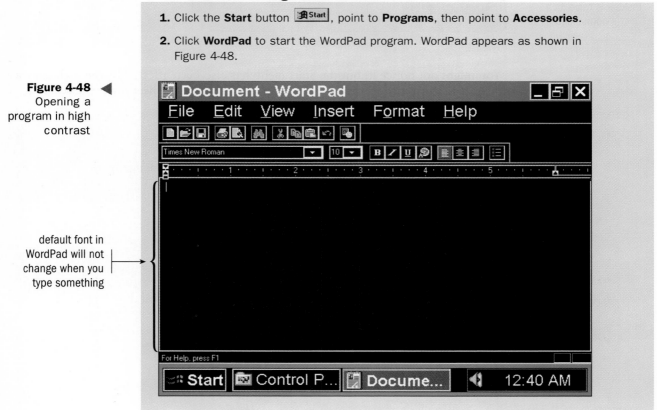

3. Type your name, and notice that the default font in WordPad itself does not change when high contrast is active.

4. Click the **Close** button ☒ to close WordPad.

5. Click the **No** button when you are asked if you want to save the document.

You shouldn't leave the desktop display in high-contrast mode if you are in a computer lab at your school. Restore the desktop to its original appearance. When you turn off high contrast, you'll find that the taskbar is larger than it should be. You can easily restore it to its normal size by dragging its top border down.

To turn off the high-contrast setting:

1. Click the **Use High Contrast** check box to remove the check mark.

2. Click the **Apply** button to apply the new setting. After a short time the screen returns to the normal display.

TROUBLE? If the Apply button is hidden behind the taskbar, drag the title bar of the Accessibility window up until you can see the Apply button.

3. To return the taskbar to its normal height, position the pointer over the top edge of the taskbar as shown in Figure 4-49, then drag the top edge of the task bar down to the normal height and release the mouse button.

Figure 4-49 ◀
Resizing the
taskbar

taskbar is twice its
normal size

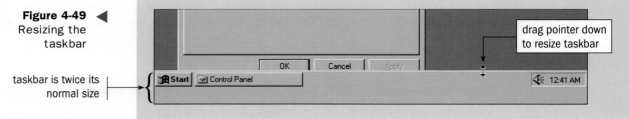

You might not notice it, but the Start menu has also been affected by the high-contrast settings. To return it to its original size, you use the property sheet for the taskbar.

To restore the Start menu to its original size:

1. Right-click a blank area of the taskbar, then click Properties.

2. Click the **Show small icons in Start menu** check box, then click the **Apply** button. See Figure 4-50.

Figure 4-50 ◄
Restoring Start
menu icons

changes to small
icons when selected

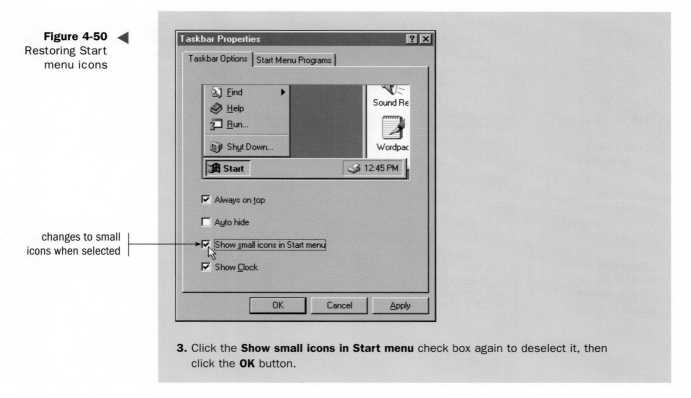

3. Click the **Show small icons in Start menu** check box again to deselect it, then click the **OK** button.

It might seem strange that you must first reduce the icons to their smallest size before you can return them to the default size. There is no other easy way to restore the Start menu to its original size.

Turning Off Accessibility Options Automatically

You can set Accessibility Options to turn off automatically after the computer sits idle for a specified period of time. This is ideal for situations such as computer labs where you want to use accessibility options but other users don't. You can activate an accessibilty option, and when you're done, Windows 95 automatically turns it off if the computer sits idle for a period of time.

To make sure that Accessibility Options turn off after a specified period of time:

1. Click the **General** tab in the Accessibility Properties dialog box.

2. If the **Turn off accessibility features after idle for:** check box is not checked, click it to activate this feature.

3. You can click the **minutes** list arrow to select a period of time from 5 to 30 minutes after which the accessibility features automatically turn off. Study Figure 4-51 to see how you would make sure that the accessibility features turn off after a specified period of time. Don't make this change, however, if you are using a lab computer.

Figure 4-51 ◀
Idling
accessibility
options

turns accessibility
options off when
selected

select number of
minutes of idle time
before accessibility
options disengage

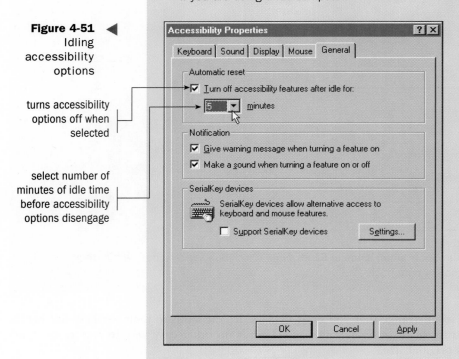

4. Click the **OK** button to close the Accessibility Properties dialog box.

5. Click the Control Panel button in the taskbar, then close the Control Panel window.

Quick Check

1 You change most mouse settings using the Control Panel mouse icon. What mouse setting can you change using the Mouse property sheet in the Accessibility Options dialog box?

2 If you set the mouse for left-handed use, what happens when you click an icon with the left mouse button?

3 Name two settings you can change to make it easier to use Windows 95 if you have limited vision.

4 If you are using MouseKeys, what number on the numeric keypad should you press when you want to select an object?

5 What keyboard shortcut opens the Start menu?

6 What modifier key do you use to open a menu?

End Note

Beth is impressed with the degree of customization possible with Windows 95. After working with the document-centric desktop she created for herself, she realizes that trivial as they may seem, the icons on the desktop increase productivity enormously. She never fails to log a phone call because the phone log is immediately available. She can access her drives, documents, and printer more easily than ever. Moreover, clients have commented on the professional look of the office desktops, and with her new skills Beth plans to use a bitmap of a favorite mountain scene as her home computer desktop background. She's also confident that she could customize one of the Companions computers for any of her employees with special needs.

One of the most exciting features of Windows 95 is the way it lends itself to the needs of its users. Although your ability to customize Windows 95 in a lab setting is limited, and is most likely to be changed by the next user, if you are running Windows 95 on your own computer, you will find that designing a desktop that reflects your needs is time well spent. In creating a document-centric desktop you should keep one thing in mind: too many icons on the desktop defeats the purpose of giving quick access to your documents. If you have icons crowded all over the desktop, it is difficult to locate quickly the one you want.

Tutorial Assignments

1. **Creating Shortcuts** Use Quick Format to format your Student Disk, then make a new Student Disk. Use the Windows 95 New Perspectives Introductory option on the CTI Windows 95 Applications menu (the files you worked with in Tutorial 3). Start Windows Explorer. First create a shortcut to the printer you use regularly. Then create a shortcut to the Beckman text document on your Student Disk. Drag the Beckman shortcut icon to the printer shortcut to print the Beckman document. When you are finished, delete both icons from your desktop.

2. **Customizing a Desktop at Highland Yearbooks** You provide computer support at Highland Yearbooks, a company that publishes high school and college yearbooks. Highland has just upgraded to Windows 95, and you'd like to get right to work customizing the desktops of Highland employees for optimal performance. You start with the computer belonging to John McPhee, one of the sales representatives. Create a desktop for John that takes the following circumstances into account. When you are done, print an image of the desktop using the techniques you learned in the previous tutorial. Then make sure you remove any shortcuts you created and restore the desktop to its original settings. Write down which options you changed to meet John's needs on the back of your printout.
    a. John keeps a Notepad file with a time-date stamp of long-distance phone calls stored on a floppy disk.
    b. John wants to be able to print the phone log file quickly without having to open it first.
    c. The company colors at Highland Yearbooks are blue and gold. John would like a blue desktop with gold title bars.
    d. John recently slammed the car door on his fingers and would like to avoid using the mouse until the bruises have healed.

3. **Create a Shortcut to a Folder** Beth recently assigned an undergraduate at one of the local colleges, Sally Hanson, to provide housekeeping for three clients. Sally plans to be out of the area over spring break, so Beth needs to write a memo to each client asking if they need replacement help. Beth would like to be able to get at the correspondence for Sally Hanson more easily.
    a. Start Windows Explorer, then create a new folder called "Sally" on your Student Disk.
    b. Start Notepad, then compose the three memos, typing in your own message as the text. Save the memos to the Sally folder on your Student Disk with the names "Smith," "Arruga," and "Kosta" (the names of the three clients). Close Notepad when you are finished.

c. Drag the Sally folder from Windows Explorer to the desktop using the right mouse button, then click Create Shortcut(s) Here.

d. Name the shortcut icon "Sally."

e. Test the shortcut icon by opening the Sally folder, then open one of the memos. Use two different methods to open these two objects, and write down which methods you used.

f. Arrange your desktop so you can see the open memo in Notepad, the open folder window, and the shortcut icon. You might need to resize the windows to make them smaller. Then print an image of the desktop using the techniques you learned in the previous tutorial.

g. Remove the shortcut to the folder when you are done.

4. **Customizing the Mouse** One of Beth's older clients, Antonio Castagna, would like part-time work at the offices of Companions, Inc. helping prepare client schedules. Beth wants to make the mouse easier for him to use. She asks you to adjust the double-click speed and pointer speed to their lowest settings. Print images of the two property sheets you use to do this using the techniques you learned in Tutorial 3. Restore the settings to their original speed when you are finished.

5. **Exploring Accessibility Options** This tutorial didn't use the FilterKeys and ToggleKeys options on the Keyboard property sheet in the Accessibility Options dialog box. Explore these options. Click the Help button (the question mark **?** in the upper-right corner of the dialog box) and then click these two items on the property sheet to discover what they do. Write a paragraph describing the circumstances under which you'd use these settings.

6. **Create a New Bitmap on the Desktop** In this tutorial you created a new text document directly on the desktop. In this tutorial assignment, you'll create an icon on the desktop for a new bitmap image. Once you've created the icon, you'll open the bitmap image and use the mouse to write your signature. Then you'll use this bitmap image as the wallpaper on your desktop.

a. Right-click an empty area of the desktop, point to New, then click Bitmap Image.

b. Name the new icon "My Signature."

c. Open My Signature. What program does Windows 95 use to open this file?

d. Drag the mouse over the empty canvas to write your signature, as shown in Figure 4-52.

Figure 4-52 ◀

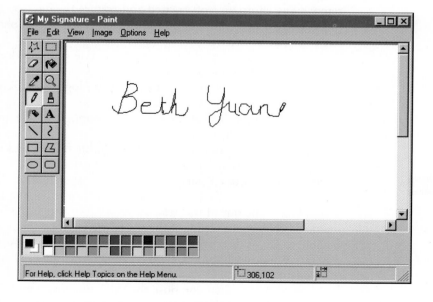

e. Exit the program, and save your changes.

f. Right-click an empty area of the desktop, click Properties, then make sure the Background property sheet is visible. Arrange the dialog box so you can see the My Signature icon.

g. Drag the My Signature icon into the Wallpaper list box, as shown in Figure 4-53.

Figure 4-53 ◀

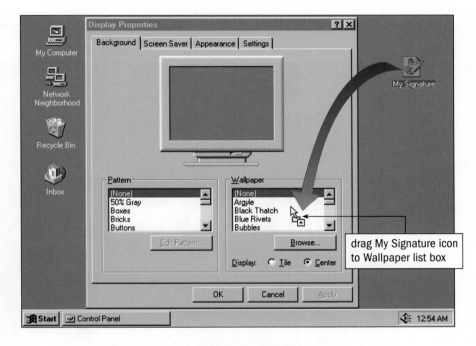

h. Click the OK button. Your signature appears as the wallpaper. Print an image of the screen using the techniques you learned in Tutorial 3.

i. Restore the desktop to its original appearance by returning the Wallpaper setting to None in the Background property sheet (make sure you click OK), and then deleting the My Signature icon from the desktop.

7. **Explore Your Computer's Desktop Properties** Answer each of the following questions about the desktop properties on your lab computers. You can find all the answers in the Display Properties dialog box, which you can reach by right-clicking an empty area of the desktop and then clicking Properties.

a. What is your monitor type? Click the Change Display Type button on the Settings property sheet to find out. Is your monitor Energy Star compliant?

b. If your monitor is Energy Star compliant, is it running any of the Windows 95 energy-saving features? Which ones?

c. What is the setting for monitor resolution? What other resolution settings are available? Drag the slider to find out. If it's an older monitor, it might not have higher resolutions available.

d. What color palette are you using?

e. Is Windows 95 using a screen saver? Which one? After how many minutes of idle time does it engage?

f. What is your desktop's default color scheme?

g. Does your desktop display a pattern or wallpaper? Which one?

8. **Customizing Your Desktop** The ability to place icons directly on the desktop gives you the opportunity to create a truly document-centric desktop. Figure 4-54 shows Beth's desktop after she's had a chance to create all the shortcuts you recommended and add additional shortcuts for programs, folders, files, and other resources she uses regularly.

Figure 4-54 ◀

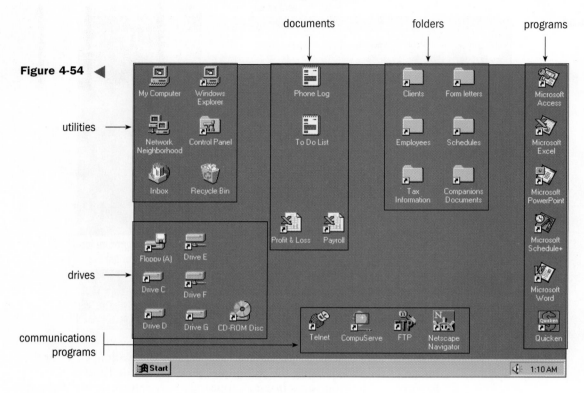

Notice that this desktop has shortcuts for not just drives and documents, but also for programs, utilities, and other Windows 95 objects. The amount of time you save by arranging your desktop in this manner cannot be overestimated if you spend a lot of time at the computer. If you have your own computer, create a desktop that meets your needs.

Use the following strategy:

a. Use Windows Explorer to locate the drives on your computer, then create a shortcut to each drive.

b. If you haven't already, use Windows Explorer to create folders for the work you usually do on your computer. You might want a folder for each class you're taking, letters you write, projects, or hobbies. Then create a shortcut to each folder you use regularly.

c. Create shortcuts for each document you use repeatedly. Remember not to overcrowd your desktop.

d. If you know how to locate program and utility files, create shortcuts to the programs and utilities you use most often.

e. Group the icons on your desktop so that similar objects are in the same location.

Answers to Quick Check Questions

SESSION 1.1

1. a. icon b. Start button c. taskbar d. Date/Time control e. desktop f. pointer

2. Multitasking

3. Start menu

4. Lift up the mouse, move it to the right, then put it down, and slide it left until the pointer reaches the left edge of the screen.

5. Highlighting

6. If a program is running, its button is displayed on the taskbar.

7. Each program that is running uses system resources, so Windows 95 runs more efficiently when only the programs you are using are open.

8. Answer: If you do not perform the shut down procedure, you might lose data.

SESSION 1.2

1. a. title bar b. program title c. Minimize button d. Restore button e. Close button f. menu bar g. toolbar h. formatting bar i. status bar j. taskbar k. workspace l. pointer

2. a. Minimize button—hides the program so only its button is showing on the taskbar.
   b. Maximize button—enlarges the program to fill the entire screen.
   c. Restore button—sets the program to a pre-defined size.
   d. Close button—stops the program and removes its button from the taskbar.

3. a. Ellipses—indicate a dialog box will appear.
   b. Grayed out—the menu option is not currently available.
   c. Submenu—indicates a submenu will appear.
   d. Check mark—indicates a menu option is currently in effect.

4. Toolbar

5. a. scroll bar b. scroll box c. Cancel button d. down arrow button e. list box f. radio button g. check box

6. one, check boxes

7. On-line Help

SESSION 2.1

1. file

2. formatting

3. I-beam

4. insertion point

5. word wrap

6. You drag the I-beam pointer over the text to highlight it.

7. \ ? : * < > | "

8. extension

9. save the file again

10. paper

SESSION 2.2

1. My Computer

2. A (or A:)

3. Hard (or hard disk)

4. Filename, file type, file size, date, time

5. Root

6. Folders (or subdirectories)

7. It is deleted from the disk.

8. Yes

SESSION 3.1

1. Windows Explorer

2. Folders, Contents

3. F

4. F

5. subfolder

6. plus box

7. Drive A device icon

8. F

SESSION 3.2

1. T

2. device or folder icon

3. F

4. Details

5. Large Icons, Small Icons, List, Details

6 Shift, Ctrl

7 Modified

8 Windows 95 temporarily stores an image of the screen in memory. You can then paste the image into an accessory like WordPad and print it.

SESSION 3.3

1 When you use the left mouse button, the pop-up menu does not appear, so you might lose track of whether you are moving or copying files.

2 Refresh

3 T

4 T

5 F

SESSION 4.1

1 F

2 F

3 Here are three ways: 1) Click the document icon with the left mouse button then press Enter, 2) Right-click the document icon then click Open, and 3) Double-click the document icon.

4 You delete not only the icon but also the document.

5 You delete only the icon but not the document.

6 You place a copy of the document on the desktop rather than placing a shortcut to the original document.

SESSION 4.2

1 F

2 Right-click the object then click Properties.

3 Here are four: Background, Appearance, Screen Saver, or Settings. You could also mention the properties on each of these sheets, like the color palette, the resolution, and so on.

4 Activate a screen saver

5 There are 640 pixels across and 480 down.

6 640 × 480, because it displays the largest objects.

7 It requires extra video memory and runs more slowly.

8 Energy Star compliant

SESSION 4.3

1. MouseKeys, which lets you use the number keys on the keypad to take over the function of the mouse.

2. You select the icon.

3. Pointer trails and high contrast

4. 5

5. Ctrl+Esc

6. Alt

Index

Microsoft Windows 95 **Task Reference**

TASK	PAGE #	RECOMMENDED METHOD	NOTES
Accessibility Options, open	130	Open Control Panel, open (might need to install with Add/Remove programs)	
Accessibility Options, turn off automatically	139	Open Accessibility Options, click General tab, click Turn off accessibility features after idle for, select number of minutes, click OK	
Character, delete	33	Press Backspace	
Check box, de-select	21	Click the check box again	Tab to option, press Spacebar
Check box, select	21	Click the checkbox	Tab to option, press Spacebar
Color palette, change	123	Right-click desktop, click Settings, click new color palette, click OK, then follow prompts to reboot computer	
Computer, view devices and folders	62	From Windows Explorer, scroll the Folders list	
Control Panel, open	125	Click **Start**, point to Settings, click Control Panel	See "Using the Control Panel to Customize Settings"
Desktop document, creating	98	Right-click desktop, point to New, click document type	See "Creating a New Document on the Desktop"
Desktop, change background	112	Right-click desktop, click Properties, click Background, click pattern or wallpaper, click OK	
Desktop, change colors	116	Right-click desktop, click Properties, click Appearance, click item, click a color, click OK	
Detailed file list, view	45	From My Computer, click View, Details	
Disk, copy your	50	Place disk in drive A:, from My Computer click , click File, Copy Disk, Start	See "Making a Backup of Your Floppy Disk."
Disk, format	30	Click , click , press Enter, click File click Format, click Start	
Disk, Quick format	58	From My Computer, click disk icon, click File, click Format, Click Quick (erase) button, click Start	
Drop-down list, display	20	Click	
Energy-saving features, use	124	Right-click desktop, click Screen Saver, click energy saving options, click OK	
File, copy		From My Computer, right-click the file, drag to the new location, press C	
File, copy in Windows Explorer	83	Drag file from Contents list to new location in Folders list using the right mouse button, then click Copy Here	Ctrl+drag the object, See "Copying One or More Files"

Microsoft Windows 95 **Task Reference**

TASK	PAGE #	RECOMMENDED METHOD	NOTES
File, delete	49	From My Computer, click the file, press Delete, click Yes	See "Deleting a File."
File, move	48	From My Computer, use the left mouse button to drag the file to the desired folder or drive	See "Moving a File."
File, move in Windows Explorer	81	Drag file from Contents list to new location in Folders list using the right mouse button, then click Move Here	Shift+drag the object, See "Moving One or More Files Between Folders"
File, open	37	Click 📂	
File, print	39	Click 🖨	
File, print preview	39	Click 🔍	
File, rename	49	From My Computer, click the file, click File, click Rename, type new name, press Enter	See "Renaming a File."
File, save	35	Click 💾	
File or folder, rename	67	Click file or folder, click label, type new name, then press Enter	F2, See "Renaming a Folder"
Files, arrange	72	Click the Name, Size, Type, or Modified button	See "Arranging Files by Name, Size, Date, or Type"
Files, select all but one	77	Select the files you don't want selected, then click File, click Invert Selection	See "Selecting all Files Except Certain Ones"
Files, select in groups	75	Click Edit, click Select All for all, press Shift then click first and last for consecutive, or press Ctrl then click files one at a time for non-consecutive	Ctrl+A to select all, See "Selecting Files"
Files, view details	72	▦	
Files, view in Windows Explorer	71	Click 📁 in Folders list	
Folder, create	46	From My Computer, click File, New, Folder	See "Creating a New Folder."
Folder, create in Windows Explorer	66	From Windows Explorer, click File, click New, click Folder	See "Creating a Folder in Windows Explorer"
Folder or device, select	64	From Windows Explorer, click 📁 or device icon	See "Selecting a Device or Folder"
Folder or device, view or hide contents	63	From Windows Explorer, click ➕ to view; ➖ to hide	Right arrow to view, left arrow to hide, See "Expanding Devices or Folders in the Folders List"
Help topic, display	23	From the Help Contents window, click the topic, then click Open	
Help topic, open	23	From the Help Contents window, click the book, then click Display	

Microsoft Windows 95 **Task Reference**

TASK	PAGE #	RECOMMENDED METHOD	NOTES
Help, start	21	Click **Start**, then click Help	F1, See "Starting Windows 95 Help."
High contrast, enable	136	Open Accessibility Options, click Display tab, click Use High Contrast, click OK	
Icon, open	43	Click the icon, then press Enter or double-click the icon	See "Opening an Icon."
Icons, view large	45	From My Computer, click View, Large Icons	
Insertion point, move	34	Click the desired location in the document Use arrow keys	
Keyboard shortcuts, perform with StickyKeys	134	Open Accessibility Options, click Keyboard tab, click Use StickyKeys, click OK	
List box, scroll	20	Click ▲ or ▼, or drag the scroll box	
Menu option, select	17	Click the menu option	
Menu, open		Click the menu option	Alt-underlined letter
Mouse pointer, control with keyboard	131	Open Accessibility Options, click Mouse tab, click Use MouseKeys, click OK	
Mouse, adjust double-click speed	128	Open Control Panel, open Mouse, click Buttons tab, drag Double-click speed slider to new location, click OK.	
Mouse, adjust pointer speed	130	Open Control Panel, open Mouse, click Motion tab, drag Pointer speed slider to new location, click OK	
Mouse, configure for right or left hand	126	Open Control Panel, open Mouse, click Buttons tab, click Right-handed or Left-handed, click OK	
Mouse, turn on pointer trails	129	Open Control Panel, open Mouse, click Motion tab, click Show pointer trails, click OK	
Object menu, open	97	Right-click object	Shift+F10
Program, quit	10	Click ✕	Alt-F4
Program, start	9	Click the Start button, point to Programs, to the program option, click the program	See "Starting a Program."
Properties, view	110	Right-click object, click Properties	Alt+Enter, See "Viewing and Changing Object Properties"
Radio button, de-select	21	Click a different radio button	Tab to option, press Spacebar
Radio button, select	21	Click the radio button	Tab to option, press Spacebar
Resolution, change	120	Right-click desktop, click Settings, drag Desktop area slider to new resolution, click OK	

Microsoft Windows 95 **Task Reference**

TASK	PAGE #	RECOMMENDED METHOD	NOTES
Screen saver, activate	118	Right-click desktop, click Screen Saver, click a screen saver, click OK	
Screen, print	78	Press Print Screen, start WordPad, click 🖨, click 💾	See "Printing the Exploring Window"
Shortcut, create on the desktop	102	Drag object's icon to desktop with the right mouse button, then click Create Shortcut(s) here	See "Creating a Shortcut"
Shortcut, delete	109	Click shortcut icon, press Delete, click Yes	
Start menu, display			Ctrl-Esc
Student data disk, create	41	Click ⏴Start, click Programs, CTI Win95, Windows 95 Brief, Make Windows 95 Student Disk, press Enter	
Text, select	34	Drag the pointer over the text	
Time-date stamp, insert on Notepad document	100	Type .LOG in uppercase letters at beginning of Notepad document	
Toolbar, view	69	Click View, click Toolbar	
Tooltip, display	19	Position pointer over the tool	
Window, change size	17	Drag ▨	
Window, close	10	Click ☒	Ctrl-F4
Window, maximize	17	Click ☐	
Window, minimize	15	Click ▁	
Window, move	17	Drag the title bar	
Window, redisplay	16	Click the taskbar button	
Window, refresh view	88	Click View, click Refresh	F5
Window, restore	16	Click ▣	
Window, switch	12	Click the taskbar button of the program	Alt-Tab, See "Switching Between Programs."
Windows Explorer, adjust list width	68	Point at dividing bar between lists so pointer changes to ◀|▶, then drag dividing bar right or left	See "Adjusting the Width of the Folders List"
Windows Explorer, open	61	Click ⏴Start, click Programs, click Windows Explorer	
Windows 95, shut down	12	Click ⏴Start, click Shut Down, Click Yes	
Windows 95, start	5	Turn on the computer	